OMG this book is so me! I always say a day is wasted without laughter. The tips and stories shared by Ed, Mark & Nicky in this book will help you to live a life filled with more fun, joy and enthusiasm... who doesn't want more of that!!?
Alison Hammond, TV Presenter

Kids are so authentic and there's no reason for us to lose that when we're older. Kids see the wonder and awe in the smallest things every day. The concept and practical suggestions in *Be More Kid* remind us how important it is to bring out the best in ourselves and how we can do that in way that also brings out the best in others.
Ben Shephard, TV Presenter

This book gives you the tools to bring the belief, energy and passion you had as a child into your current life with transformational results.
Sarah Stirk, TV Presenter, Sky Sports & Entrepreneur

As a kid growing up in Birmingham, all I wanted to do was become a chef and have the most successful restaurant in Birmingham. This book reminds us of the important things that make us happy, and it gives down to earth, practical advice to make sure we are being true to who we really are and living our own dreams.
Glynn Purnell, (the Yummy Brummie)
Michelin-starred chef

This concept really works well both personally and in business. It's what we've built the HDY Culture on and is the glue that binds us together.
Geoff Percy, Non-Exec Chair of HDY Agency,
SLG and H Bronnley.co.uk

Be More Kid is a completely fresh approach to personal development that aligns with my passion for health and fitness. Never underestimate the positive effect that playing and having fun can add to both life and͏   ͏ryday - they've

:nade

D1393293

BE MORE KID

BE
MORE
KID

ED JAMES
MARK TAYLOR
NICKY TAYLOR

BE
MORE
KID

HOW TO ESCAPE THE
GROWN UP TRAP AND
LIVE LIFE TO THE FULL!

CAPSTONE
A Wiley Brand

This edition first published 2021

© 2021 Mark Taylor, Nicky Taylor & Ed James

Registered office

John Wiley & Sons Ltd, The Atrium, Southern Gate, Chichester, West Sussex, PO19 8SQ, United Kingdom

For details of our global editorial offices, for customer services and for information about how to apply for permission to reuse the copyright material in this book please see our website at www.wiley.com.

Wiley publishes in a variety of print and electronic formats and by print-on-demand. Some material included with standard print versions of this book may not be included in e-books or in print-on-demand. If this book refers to media such as a CD or DVD that is not included in the version you purchased, you may download this material at http://booksupport.wiley.com. For more information about Wiley products, visit www.wiley.com.

Designations used by companies to distinguish their products are often claimed as trademarks. All brand names and product names used in this book are trade names, service marks, trademarks or registered trademarks of their respective owners. The publisher is not associated with any product or vendor mentioned in this book.

Limit of Liability/Disclaimer of Warranty: While the publisher and author have used their best efforts in preparing this book, they make no representations or warranties with respect to the accuracy or completeness of the contents of this book and specifically disclaim any implied warranties of merchantability or fitness for a particular purpose. It is sold on the understanding that the publisher is not engaged in rendering professional services and neither the publisher nor the author shall be liable for damages arising herefrom. If professional advice or other expert assistance is required, the services of a competent professional should be sought.

Library of Congress Cataloging-in-Publication Data is Available:

ISBN 9780857088833 (paperback)

ISBN 9780857088987 (epdf)

ISBN 9780857088994 (epub)

Cover Design: Wiley

Set in 11/14pt AJensonPro-Regular by SPi Global, Chennai, India

Printed in Great Britain by CPI Group (UK) Ltd, Croydon CR0 4YY

10 9 8 7 6 5 4 3 2 1

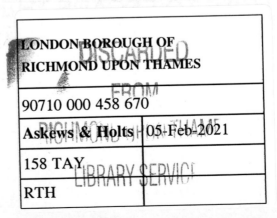

May this book speak to the child within us all
and set them free ...

CONTENTS

ACKNOWLEDGEMENTS

Without Jaime's fall (whilst unpleasant at the time), the idea for this book would never have been born, so Jaime we thank you, as your 'just get on with it' attitude has given us the vehicle to bring inspiration to so many, across the world. We also say thank you to Jack, Jacob, Andrew, Richard, Hannah and Alex for your patience whilst we learned to be parents; we know we haven't always got it right, yet our intentions have always been good.

We are grateful for the fun, curiosity and sheer enjoyment of life experienced by our grandchildren – Eithan, Jessica, Maddie, Thea, Evie and Freya – constant reminders that we all need to be more kid!

To our families, Mum, Dad, Sarah and Megan for their love, support and belief.

We express our heartfelt appreciation to all of the children who took part in our research for the book, you provided us with endless joy, listening to your views on the world; thank you also to their parents for playing your part in our research and to everyone who has openly shared with us their problems, confidences and optimism for life, we listened and we sincerely hope this book will be of benefit to you.

Thanks to everyone who has ever listened, called, texted or got in touch with Ed's radio show on Heart, your stories of playfulness, getting the most out of life and finding the fun have been a constant source of inspiration.

We include a special thank you to the team at Heart/Global for their support over the years, and putting up with Ed whilst he was working on the book!

To friends, colleagues and clients at HDY Agency, especially Angel, Geoff and John; mentors Tad and Adriana James; and the thousands of people across the world who we have helped and coached through the Taylored Life Company, we thank you for the positive impact that you have had on our lives.

Immense gratitude to Georgia Kirke for her passion, humour and guidance and for keeping us on track every single week for 6 months (no mean feat!) and helping us to turn an idea that Ed had for 10 years into this book we now call *Be More Kid!*

Many thanks also to Wiley for believing in us, right from the beginning we have loved that you share our excitement and enthusiasm for *Be More Kid!* We are grateful for the ideas that you bring, your endless support and for giving us the opportunity to share this book with so many people.

Last but not least, we are thankful for the journey that each of us has travelled, the lessons that life has taught us, the expertise that we have gained along the way and the privilege that we now have to be able to share this with others. If we are able to Make THE Difference to just one person, then we have achieved our purpose.

INTRODUCTION

As Rachael sat in the chair, she seemed to diminish in size. It was as though she had left the façade, the one she showed to the rest of the world, at the door. This was the real Rachael, the person with fears and doubts, unsure of herself and exhausted from pretending.

To her family and colleagues she appeared confident and self-assured, knowing exactly what she wanted from life and doing what was needed to make it happen. On the inside she felt far from confident, she felt as though she was never enough and she had lost her way.

She no longer knew what she wanted.

What she did know was that she was tired. She knew that to everyone else her life looked idyllic and she knew she should be grateful for what she had, but there was something missing.

What was worse was that Rachael believed that she was the only person who felt this way. Yet the previous week it had been Jo sitting there saying virtually the same thing. A couple of days before that it was Tom.

Tom had shared something he felt deeply ashamed of, something he didn't feel he could tell anyone. It was a huge weight on his shoulders. He felt as though he had suddenly woken up one day and found himself with a wife, a large mortgage, three children and an expensive car. He hated his job but he was stuck with it – he desperately needed the money – so he went to work day after day; he was bored and he felt like running away, trapped in a life he didn't enjoy.

For Jo, everything irritated her. She found herself shouting at the kids and her husband for small things that she knew weren't even important, but she couldn't seem to stop herself. She was overeating, drinking more than she knew was good for her and avoiding exercise, even though she knew she would feel better for it if she made the effort. She had started making silly mistakes at work, and she wanted to get her life back on track before it became worse than it already was.

Rachael, Tom, Jo ... and all of the others before them and who will probably follow them, their lives weren't how they wanted them to be.

As kids we have big dreams, anything and everything seems possible, and we believe that there is so much time ahead of us to achieve those dreams. Then over time we stop thinking about those dreams and ambitions, we lose the motivation and determination that we once had ... and we don't even notice it.

The great thing is that the resources we had when we were kids are still there; we've just forgotten how to use them.

In 2011, Bronnie Ware – an Australian nurse – wrote a book called *The Top Five Regrets of the Dying*. Bronnie Ware cared for people in the last 12 weeks of their life and recorded the common themes that patients had regarding regrets and what, on reflection, they would have done differently in their life. These are the five regrets that were mentioned most frequently:

1 I wish I'd had the courage to live a life true to myself, not the life others expected of me.
2 I wish I hadn't worked so hard.
3 I wish I'd had the courage to express my feelings.
4 I wish I'd stayed in touch with my friends.
5 I wish I had let myself be happier.

We have written this book, *Be More Kid: How to Escape the Grown Up Trap and Live Life to the Full*, for everyone who wants to get the very best from their life, so that no-one need have these same regrets. It's not a self-improvement book about giving up chocolate or alcohol, which you may be relieved to hear, but rather a book about changing your deeper mindset to understand what really matters to you, and being happy.

We have included practical exercises for you throughout the book. To get the most out of it, these exercises should be completed as you read through each chapter, and it's our intention that you read the book in chapter order, as each chapter builds on the previous one. There are also additional resources available on the website at www.be-more-kid.co.uk, which gives you the opportunity to download electronic copies of the full version of the exercises. You will also find additional exercises, as well as videos and access to podcasts, that focus on some of the topics discussed in the book.

Parts of the book may make you feel uncomfortable, parts may challenge your thinking – that's ok. Change means going outside of your comfort zone, and there are no wrong feelings or responses or answers. All we ask is that you have an open mind and give it a go.

Have you ever noticed how differently children react to things that might incapacitate an adult?

This story shows that it's not what happens to you, but how you react to things that determine happiness and success.

Ed's story

When my little girl was six, she broke her arm. She was playing with her brothers on the top bunk and fell off, landing badly on her arm. I still remember hearing the thud from downstairs when she landed. The reason I'm telling you this is because this is the moment that made me look at her, and in fact all kids, in a totally different light.

Back to my daughter and the starting point to this 'philosophy'. She coped incredibly. The only time she cried was when she first fell. She then handled every little thing that was thrown at her. The operation was stress-free, she enjoyed choosing a sling and cast because she was able to have her favourite colour – pink! She proudly told everyone at school what had happened and how long she'd be without the use of her arm for. In short, she not only accepted it, but totally embraced it. She opened drawers with her good arm and closed them with her head. I still have a picture of her at Disney on Ice smiling and proudly showing her pink sling off!

Comparing a child's typical response to how an adult would react in a similar situation, and contemplating other comparisons between kids and adults, we realised how many amazing resources we have as a kid that we lose touch with as we grow into adults, and how much we would all positively benefit from being able to reconnect with these resources again, combining them with the knowledge and experience that we now have as adults.

Research we've carried out over the last three years, in preparation for writing this book, has shown us that there are far too many people who are not happy; and there are a number of common reasons that they give for this.

They are not happy because they are not doing the things that are important to them, and feel guilty for wanting to. They don't have the relationships that they crave. They are yearning to be accepted for who they are, rather than feeling the need to fulfil other people's expectations. Feeling full of doubt and having self-limiting beliefs around confidence and trust, trapped by finances, in jobs and relationships that are not working for them. People feel stuck and they don't know how to free themselves.

Surely there must be more to life ... ?

When there are so many people who are so desperately unhappy, often leading them to anxiety and depression, you might question what prevents them from changing their lives?

The problem is that we are not taught how to control our emotions; we are not taught that we can actually change our thinking if it doesn't get us the outcomes we want, and we're not given the tools that we need to do that. There is a common mentality that we are not in control of our own thinking, not in control of our own lives – that things just happen to us. An attitude of blame is prevalent. The problem is that whilst we continue to absolve ourselves from responsibility and avoid being accountable as individuals, we are not the driver in our own lives, we are merely passengers, and therefore completely disempowered.

Our desired outcome for writing this book is to help you become the driver in your life, to assist you in recognising and reconnecting with some of the resources that you once had as a kid, and help you use those resources together with the knowledge and experience that you now have as an adult, to live a life that is more fulfilled and content.

Will challenges still present themselves? Yes of course! Life will still happen; yet you will be more resilient to those challenges when they do arise. And remember: if you keep doing things the same way, nothing is going to change.

We are sharing our years of expertise in human behaviour, as well as our own experiences of how we have risen to life's challenges, so that you can improve your life for the better, and to show you how you can have fun while doing it. This book is all about how to live a better life and 'Be More Kid!'

Part I

Stuck and Settling For

In January 2018 we sent out a survey to a group of adults asking them lots of different questions about their lives. The results that came back were pretty conclusive. Most people felt that they are 'stuck'.

Things weren't terrible, but there was this nagging sense that there must be something better, that they should be doing something more. Everything had become predictable, every year was the same, and people felt like they couldn't make a change. Their only solution was to numb themselves with food or alcohol, or escape with a two-week holiday once a year.

We call this the 'Grey Zone'.

The Grey Zone is the place where many of us ultimately end up because we settle for less than we know we can have. Because it's easy and comfortable. Because it's the thing that everyone does. Go to school, maybe go to university, get a job, find a partner, get married, have kids, get a dog, and play out the same years on repeat until you retire, then die. And that's your life.

Just 'good enough'. Isn't that a terrifying thought? What happened to the dreams you had when you were a kid? What about all the big things you wanted to achieve – or even the little things, like playing an instrument or learning to speak Spanish?

The real problem with the Grey Zone is that we don't feel in control. There are so many external pressures trying to keep us stuck. Advertising everywhere says we won't be complete without some new material possession or package holiday that we can't afford, so we buy it. It makes us feel good for a couple of days, and then it's straight back to the Grey Zone. It's a trap that so many of us fall into: we get promoted into the well-paid job, move into a nice house with a mortgage, buy a car on finance, live a life we can't afford … and then there's no way out.

If you begin to hate the job, well, too bad. Now you need the money to pay off the debt. To quote Fight Club: 'We buy things we don't need with money we don't have to impress people we don't like.' Sound familiar?

The end result is that we feel like passengers in our own lives, not in control, seeing ourselves running on a treadmill without knowing how to get off. The truth is that we do have control. It is totally possible to get off. In this first part we'll be bringing your attention to some of the common Grey Zone feelings, and why things are the way they are. It's important to really understand what's going on and where you're at before trying to make changes, so let's dive in.

CHAPTER 1

WHY ARE YOU CHOOSING TO BE UNHAPPY?

Something we have found that many people have in common in the Grey Zone is that they wish their lives were better, and they spend time thinking and daydreaming about how things could be different. While having dreams for the future is great, Grey Zone daydreaming is different.

It's not being excited for something you're working towards, but rather wishing for an escape from where you're at without actually doing anything about it. Or knowing that you're capable of doing something amazing, and fantasising about doing it, but then making excuses and rationalisations for why you're not trying it out – as one of our survey respondents said, 'Life's getting in the way'. Empty wishing without any real motivation or intention to take action is not getting you anywhere.

Grey Zone inhabitants don't take any action because they don't really believe that what they dream about could come true, or are terrified of failing. And many people become bitter that they don't have what they want already. They stop truly dreaming about what they could achieve, and start wishing they had already achieved it. It's a kind of giving up; resigning themselves to the comfortable grey life, while simultaneously wanting to escape.

Kids aren't like this.

Kids dream about being an astronaut, or a ballerina, or a pilot, and they really think that's what they'll be one day. There are no limitations on what's possible. They don't worry about whether they'll succeed or fail. When they play-pretend that they're an astronaut on a spaceship going to the moon, they know that it's play, but the enjoyment they get from it is as if it's real. They're not annoyed that they aren't an actual astronaut yet! Quite the opposite: for them, imagining what it would be like is motivating, it encourages them to read books on space and look through their telescope, and they feel fulfilled.

Then gradually school teaches them that trying and failing is bad – that there are wrong answers, and that it's embarrassing. Adults may well tell them that their dreams are unlikely to happen, and as they grow up they start to believe it too. We are programmed as we grow up to be filled with doubt and negativity, so that doing what we actually want and making changes to get there seems incredibly difficult. Impossible even.

Part of the work we do as coaches is to get rid of all this negative programming so that people can start to dream like they did as a child, and to start making decisions that are actually right for them so they can experience the outcomes they want.

The art of play is something that kids naturally understand, and adults often don't. It's enjoying being in the moment, and the process of getting to where you want to be, every bit as much as enjoying the end destination. It's about having fun right here, right now, as part of the journey to what you want long-term. Compare that to how most of us think: wishing that we were somewhere else, someone else, doing something else, but never believing that it's possible, whilst at the same time feeling life is unfair that you don't have it, what a paradox!. In this case, kids' thinking makes more sense. When was the last time you just let go and played like a kid?

The bottom line – the reason behind all this daydreaming – is that people want to be happy. And it's a good aspiration. There've been lots of surveys and studies about happiness over the years, and patterns are starting to emerge on what it takes. One group of researchers from Harvard[1], after looking at a lot of data over a long period of time, suggested that the secret is choosing to be happy with whatever you do, strengthening your closest relationships, steering the direction in which you want to contribute, doing more of what you're good at and taking care of yourself physically, financially and emotionally. We'll be looking at a lot of these ideas throughout the rest of the book.

The problem today is that people confuse happiness with short-term pleasure. Many of us chase hits of feel-good brain chemicals, such as dopamine, that rapidly fade away rather than building a life of deeper contentment. We're happiness machines bouncing from one external thing to another – the new car, the new partner, the new shoes; even the one-day self-development motivational event that gets you fired up but doesn't get you to actually change – never looking inward to make things better.

This is partly because we don't always know what is good for us, but also because short-term dopamine hits don't require effort. You can always stop off for a burger and fries at the drive-thru on the way home from a job where you're bored out of your mind. But long-term contentment does take work.

Exploring your decisions is a good place to start. Before making a decision, ask yourself whether it's going to only give you short-term pleasure, or contribute to your long-term happiness. Quite often you'll find that it's either one or the other. Eating a bag of doughnuts will give you a hit of dopamine, but if it makes you fat, will it contribute to your long-term happiness? Probably not.

To avoid confusion throughout the book, rather than using the word 'happiness' we'll now call the goal 'contentment', or 'peace of mind'. Because even in the best life, sometimes things suck. Terrible things outside of your control can happen. You can't be happy all day every day. But you can have a deeper sense of contentment, even on a bad day. You can get rid of the nagging voice that's

---

[1] IPSOS Global Trends Survey: Fragmentation, Cohesion & Uncertainty – this 2017 survey was conducted with 18,180 adults aged 16–64 (USA and Canada), between 12 September and 11 October 2016. The survey looked ahead to the following 12 months, at areas of life that the adults were optimistic or pessimistic about. We also utilised our own adult surveys carried out between January and October 2018.

there every morning telling you that something's not right. And you can be more happy, more of the time.

Another big factor in the age of social media is that we're constantly comparing ourselves and our levels of happiness with those of other people. We look at people's lives on Facebook and Instagram and everything seems so perfect. Perfect house, perfect dog, perfect holiday in the Bahamas.

But we're comparing our reality with their shop window. All you see is the bits they want you to see (and they may well have spent an hour just getting the photo right). You don't see all the bad parts, because of course they don't post that online. It's impossible to compare your happiness to theirs, because you have no idea how happy they are.

But even outside of social media we're plagued with the idea of 'keeping up with the Joneses'; that whatever we have is only worth something in comparison to what other people have. It's the very definition of giving control away: we can't be content if the neighbour's TV is bigger than ours. Well they can always buy a bigger TV, so I guess we'll never be content. Not a good plan!

We know of so many people who daydream about winning the lottery, reading up on lottery winners and feeling envious. But the truth is you don't need millions of pounds. In fact, having lots of money can bring new issues you never imagined. You need to actually understand what drives you, what you want to do, and what makes you fulfilled, and then what other people have in comparison makes no difference. It's an internal thing.

Look at young kids – before the age of seven or so. They'll be happy playing with a new toy, no matter what other kids have. They'll be happy playing even without any toys, just using their imagination. As a society we could definitely spend more time enjoying what we do have than wishing for what other people have.

What's the alternative to living in the Grey Zone and empty wishing? Plan your life rather than aimlessly following the expected path. Take control. Don't end up in the trap by accident, where you feel like you can't escape the life you're in and aren't sure how you even got there. And if you're in the trap already, realise that something has to change to get out of it, and the only person who can make that change is you.

The rest of this book will help you with this. We first just want to bring your attention to what is happening in so many adults' lives. Too many of us think of life as a struggle towards an eventual utopia – hoping that 'one day' things will be great. In Victorian times this was called the 'jam tomorrow' promise, where kids were told they'd be happy in heaven, but for right now they had to climb up a chimney and clean it.

In today's society, retirement is the time when people hope to be happy. And while many of us might be happier when we're finished with work, wouldn't it be better to also enjoy life for the 50 years or so of adulthood before then, while we're still fit and young?

BE MORE KID

If you want something, work towards getting it. Take responsibility for your decisions, your actions, and your peace of mind. Start today. Don't worry about failure – remember, kids don't. And this book is all about being more kid.

The following chapter will unpack 'overthinking' and why it's not good for us, as well as providing practical tips on how you can focus your thinking in a productive way instead.

CHAPTER 2

OVERTHINKING

Many people have a tendency to overthink. Your brain races away and whatever perceived problem you have, you make it 100 times worse. You start thinking, 'What does that mean?' And you fall into the trap of thinking, 'If that happens, then this will happen, and then this could happen'. Before you know it, you've created a scenario in your mind that ends in a horrendous way. You get more anxious about it, become more stressed and then everything seems more bleak and hopeless.

It becomes a self-fulfilling prophecy. Overthinking isn't reacting to an event, it's reacting to an interpretation of an event and all the other events that follow.

Think about how differently you dealt with events when you were a child. Things happen when you're young and you react to them, but you react in the moment and take them at face value. You don't know if it's good or bad, you just know that it's happened and you go with it. You accept it. In fact, it's what we call underthinking.

As we move into adulthood, we overcomplicate things. People get sucked into the spiral of 'what ifs' and our beliefs and the values that have been imposed on us come into play. Rather than dealing with things in isolation, it's easy to get bogged down by overthinking and this makes our lives far too complicated.

People also have a tendency to focus on the things they don't want to happen. Often, by the time their thoughts have spiralled out of control, they've forgotten what the actual event was and are instead focusing on the myriad of potential negative outcomes.

We call this 'paralysis by analysis'. You get so caught up in analysing things because you're looking for certainty. Overthinking is actually a function that's designed to give you certainty and security. People do it because they want the certainty that things will be okay. But all overthinking actually does is stop them from doing anything.

THE PHYSIOLOGY OF OVERTHINKING

Overthinking is more than a mental process. When we overthink, there are physiological processes happening in our brains and our bodies.

It puts your body in stress mode. All of the neurological activity firing in your brain as you go down that overthinking spiral puts your body on high alert. You can go into fight or flight mode, which is imagined through overthinking. You aren't thinking about the original event now; you are thinking about your thinking, it's 10 to the power of 20 of the original event.

The fear takes over and your body reacts. It produces adrenaline; your heart starts beating faster, which sends more blood to your muscles. Your breathing becomes fast and shallow, so you can take in more air. Your blood sugar spikes. Your senses become heightened. You may tremble and your hands may become sweaty. This is what people often call a panic attack.

Adrenaline is only a short-lived thing. The body can get rid of adrenaline quite quickly, and it does. But when people are stressed and their minds are going ten to the dozen, they put their bodies into artificial flight mode. The body chemically reacts to that, also producing cortisol. Their physiology changes. But unlike adrenaline, the body can't get rid of cortisol quickly.

The main issue with cortisol is that it weakens your immune system. It may cause health issues such as increased blood pressure and sugar, acne and decreased libido. It can contribute to obesity and more. It's why people who are under stress and overthinking in everyday life tend to get ill. The body's physiological reaction to overthinking has a direct physical impact, it's not just in the mind. It's why people often find that they get ill as soon as they stop. The body relaxes but the immune system is weakened because it's been under stress for so long.

Many people have experienced this. It's why you always seem to come down with something when you take a week off work. Or why teachers often get sick as soon as the school holidays start.

IT MIGHT NEVER HAPPEN

Too many people worry about things that may never happen. It's exhausting to spend your life worrying about 'what ifs'. Brexit was a good example of this. No one could predict what was going to happen. With or without a deal? Whatever that outcome, the eventual effect on everyone's lives is largely unpredictable. But instead of realising there's nothing that we can do about situations like these and moving on with our lives, many people worry, overthink and create stress for themselves.

What we need to re-learn is how to react in the moment, ask ourselves what we can control and let the rest go. Be more kid and underthink things rather than overthinking things.

LETTING YOUR PAST RULE YOUR FUTURE

One of the problems with overthinking is that adults imagine pain in a situation. They anticipate that something will be painful, either physically or emotionally, and this perceived pain prevents them from doing things.

For example, they might be fearful of starting a new relationship if they've been hurt in the past. This reaction to events based on their past experiences changes the course of their lives in a negative way. They lose the ability to see things on their own merit and this prevents them from doing things in the future.

People also take things from the past that have gone wrong and use that as a benchmark as to how things are likely to turn out in the future. This in turn makes them fearful and again prevents them from doing things.

Some people will get lost inside themselves more than others. People who are what we'd call heavily auditory digital have an intense internal dialogue. They are often detached from their feelings, which can sometimes be a safety mechanism to prevent them from experiencing hurt or emotional pain. As a result, they often get caught up in their own heads, continually processing things internally without any external check. This exacerbates the stress and worry that comes with overthinking.

They have a tendency to believe that everyone else has the answer and that they're the only ones who don't get it or are missing out. This belief impacts their behaviour and how they live their lives. To break this cycle we need to unlearn overthinking.

Now Your Turn: Unlearning overthinking

For one week, be completely aware and conscious in the moment. Whatever happens during that week, train yourself to absolutely accept it. You might get stuck in traffic, or you're late for work because your alarm doesn't go off, or your child gets expelled from school (hopefully not!). Whatever it is, however big or small, say to yourself 'that's fine' and then handle it.

Look at each event and ask yourself: 1. 'Is there anything I can do about this?' Then ask yourself: 2. 'Is there anything I can influence about this?' If the answer to one or both of those questions is 'no', let go of that event.

If you have no influence over the event then you have to tell yourself that you've done the best you can. Accept what has happened and move on from there.

The idea is to change your focus and react in a more positive way. You will find the full version of this exercise at www.be-more-kid.com.

ESCAPISM VS. REPROGRAMMING

Mindfulness and meditation are very appealing, yet not as easy or effective as most people initially think. The aim of mindfulness is to give people permission to live in the way that they want to, being carefree and in the moment like a child. But most people struggle with being mindful. Meditation is something that many people give up on after a few attempts. It can take people about 20 years to learn how to meditate properly. It's not a quick fix.

The biggest issue for us is that, while mindfulness and meditation can be useful tools, they don't address the root cause of why you overthink. When you stop being mindful or stop meditating and open your eyes, your life is still the same, with the same issues and triggers that cause you to overthink.

Another way people deal with overthinking is to self-medicate. That might be with alcohol, drugs or sleeping tablets. Whatever it is, it's a way of escaping. How many people do you know who live for the weekend? They see those two days off as their chance to 'escape'.

None of these tactics deals with the root cause, and so you might escape for a while but then you just go back to the spiral of overthinking. What you need to do is identify the root cause of your overthinking and re-programme your brain. You have to re-learn how to deal with the things that happen in your life in a positive way.

FEELINGS OF DIS-EASE

Most people care about what other people think of them. It's important for people to see them as a nice person. What's interesting is the research that's been done on why that's so important for people. Various pieces of research have found that it comes down to an underlying desire to be accepted socially.

In some cases, a desire for acceptance has caused people to go against what they believe is right for them as a person. They will do things and overthink things to make themselves fit into situations that just aren't right for them.

All of this adds to the feeling of stress and a general feeling of not being at ease with themselves. The effect of this overthinking on the body can be dis-ease.

Your mind doesn't have time to switch off and be creative. You're constantly bombarded with information in the form of emails, texts, social media posts. All of this sensory overload creates stress in the body, which leads to angst and worry.

This isn't helped by the fact that there's negativity everywhere you look. It's really hard not to overthink when you're bombarded with all this negativity. Take the news, for example. Some people have it on all the time and end up worrying about everything. They take it all on and believe that it's their issue to solve.

But in reality there's nothing you can do. This returns us to the idea of asking what's within your control. If the answer is none of it, turn it off and forget about it. Don't keep looking at something on social media if it's upsetting you. If you share it and tell people that you're outraged, annoyed, scared or angry about what you've seen, all you're doing is perpetuating those feelings, both internally and to your friends.

There's a part of our brain called the reticular activating system (RAS). It's our programme to seek similarity. It's why you think you're the only person in your area who will have a particular model of car until you buy it and then you notice that every other person is driving one. Or why, when women get pregnant, more people in their lives seem to be pregnant. We're designed to seek similarity and familiarity.

That means if you're surrounded by bad news, your brain will look to find bad news automatically, because that's how you are programming yourself. This also applies to who and what you surround yourself with in your life, as well as the environment you put yourself in. All of this is crucial to what goes on in your life. As children we often grow up in this 'no-bad-news' zone, but then as adults we plunge ourselves into a world filled with negativity.

BE MORE KID

Kids don't actually have a sense of what's happening in the world. As adults, we have a tendency to shield them from anything bad, so they don't have these negative influences and they're better for it.

When you're an adult, it's almost as though you've been programmed to seek out this negativity for reassurance or safety, but all it does is make us worse. There's no need to focus on it to the extent that we do.

We also forget about the joy of 'maybe'. There's a taxi driver who we know in India, who has become well known to our graduates as we speak about him in our trainings, the famous Mr Amir. If you have a conversation with him and ask his opinion on anything, his response will always include 'maybe'. If you ask him: 'Mr Amir, is it going to rain later?' his response will be along the lines of: 'Maybe. I don't think so. Some sun, but maybe a chance of rain later, but maybe not.'

He lives a life of maybe. But most adults don't. They crave certainty and they look for it wherever they can find it. Because this certainty often comes from places like the news, it makes the focus negative. They're fed their need for certainty from the media and their environment at random.

But if you think about news reporters, really they're actually just repeaters. The majority of journalists will go into the House of Commons, listen to something and then come outside and say, 'In the House of Commons, Mr X said so and so …' They repeat what they've heard whether it's true or not, and often not in context. But the trouble is, because it's been on the news it takes on truth and is given authority.

We have a tendency to take on all the bad stuff in the world and we think we have to take it on and experience it personally. We believe we have to find a solution for it. But we don't. We shouldn't take this on. This comes back to the exercise earlier in the chapter. Can you influence it? No? Well, in that case, just move on.

CHAPTER 3

PROCRASTINATING

'Someone, somewhere with less talent and fewer qualifications than you is doing what you want to do.'

Procrastination is very often the result of overthinking. Even when someone wants to do what's important to them, the worry and fear that comes from overthinking creates conflict. This then stops them doing what they want to do. They don't want to make a decision in case they get it wrong.

But procrastination is the destroyer of our goals and dreams. It's the grave-yard of the best ideas. It's what eats at us and stops us getting what we want from our lives and what stops us doing what we want with our lives. Procrastination is a state of being stuck. You're not moving forward, you're often wallowing in self-pity and avoidance or you're just putting things off.

WHY DO PEOPLE PROCRASTINATE?

Procrastination is common if someone is feeling out of control or overwhelmed with things. When the things you need to tackle in life seem so big, or there are so many of them, it can be difficult to find a place to start. Many people procrastinate because they lose sight of the outcome.

Sometimes this can be linked to organisation – or a lack of organisation. When someone isn't organised they can't see a way forward, so they procrastinate.

Often, people will only be moved into action at the 11th hour. They've got an exam the next morning, or a speech to give the next day, or whatever it might be. It's only when that's looming that they actually do something. That means they're forced to stop procrastinating and that's their answer to the problem.

But that's very stressful and therefore has a negative impact on the body. The physiological side of stress that we talked about in the last section comes into play and that's bad for us. The other problem with this approach to procrastination is that people often don't get the outcome they want as they're forcing themselves to do something because they have to. That means whatever task it is, it's not being done with thought and preparation. Instead, they're just doing it to get away from what they don't want.

There can be other signs of procrastination that also have a negative effect on people's wellbeing. Comfort eating is often a sign of procrastination. Because people procrastinate they don't move on, and that in turn leads to feeling empty inside because they know they're not doing something that they should be doing. They can try to fill this emptiness with food. They're trying to find something comforting to make that nagging feeling go away, but unfortunately procrastination will keep nagging at you.

Fear also leads to procrastination. People can be scared of failing, but they can also be scared of succeeding because that often takes them into unknown territory. And people are scared of the unknown. Some people use delaying tactics because they don't want to know what the outcome will be, because that will often lead to change. Often the underlying cause is a lack of confidence in themselves or their abilities, or both.

THE BUSYNESS TRAP

Often people get caught in a cycle of procrastination and overthinking. If they have busy lives with a lot of things going on, they're often not organised. This lack of organisation only makes it worse and means that they procrastinate even more, so it just goes round in a cycle.

It's common to feel as though the busyness of your life is relentless. Maybe you're trying to coordinate your own life with that of your children and your partner. You've got to work, make sure everyone has dinner on the table, do the housework, take people to clubs or classes ... the list can go on.

One of the easiest ways to take yourself out of this is to make a to-do list of all the things that are going through your mind and that you think you need to do. Then put deadlines against them. Very often, people will think that they've got to do certain things, when actually they don't need to do them at all. It's just something they give themselves a hard time for. The act of writing all those tasks down and putting deadlines next to them can allow them to put the tasks into some kind of order.

Nicky's story

I was a single parent for a lot of the time that I was bringing up my two girls. I worked full time and every spare minute was taken up with something, not a moment to myself. But despite that, I still insisted on ironing all of the towels, socks and underwear. Why on earth did I do that? Because those were the values that were drummed into me when I was growing up. I was taught that you don't let your standards slip because where will that lead you to? We take on more things than we should because we have this belief that we should be doing them, but often we don't really know why.

SEEING THE BIG PICTURE

All too often people lose sight of the big picture. They forget what it is they're actually trying to achieve and instead get caught up in the whirlwind of everyday life. It's often why people start to have all sorts of new and exciting ideas when they go on holiday. They've lifted their heads out of their daily lives and start to ask themselves questions like, 'Why am I doing this job? I don't even enjoy it,' or they think 'Maybe there's a way to do this differently'.

But the problem is that they come back from their holiday and jump straight back on that treadmill. They return to living on a day-to-day basis most of the time.

At different points in your life different things will take on greater or lesser importance. When you have kids, your relationships or exercise regime might get a lower score. If you want to put more energy into your career, what other things will you have less time for? The key isn't to try and balance all things equally at once, or to focus on one thing and forget about the others, but to maintain the elements of your life that are important to you.

Oh, and by the way, we don't believe in the notion of 'work–life balance'. Why should work be *as* important as your life? Work is part of your life and needs considering alongside the other areas of your life, as the exercise above encourages. What you need – and what this book is helping you to create – is what we call a 'Taylored' life. You tailor it to fit what you want for that time of your life.

If there's an area that you can't dedicate lots of time to right now, accept that and do what you need to maintain it at an acceptable level to you. But don't attach any guilt to the fact that you don't go to the gym three times a week now you've got kids, for instance. Make the decision about where your focus will lie, accept it and get on with your life. If it is important, change what you are doing and accept that choice.

The following exercise can highlight areas with a lot of guilt attached to them. You feel like you should be able to be a mum or dad, have a job, keep the house in a good state, have a hobby, see your friends, go out for a drink and so on. But actually, what you need to do is really focus on your priorities right now.

If you're going to concentrate on certain things, you can't do everything else to the same extent. You need to accept this and put a plan in place so that you can maintain those other areas but keep them conscious, i.e. you are aware of them but without all the guilt and expectation.

Now Your Turn: Wheel of Life

The Wheel of Life is a way to help you plan your life so that you are able to focus on what's important. What often isn't understood is that your focus will change as you move through your life. You'll evolve and you'll evolve with different people, which is especially the case when you become a parent.

You can find a Wheel of Life that you can customise on our website www .be-more-kid.com. How it works is that you split your Wheel of Life into six to eight segments, areas that you want to focus on. That might be relationships, health, fitness, children, finances. What the segments are doesn't matter too much, but they should align with what's important to you. This is an example for you.

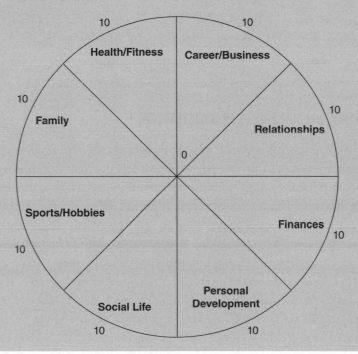

(*continued*)

Next score each category on your wheel from 0 to 10 according to how satisfied you are with each area of your life. 0 is in the centre and represents not at all satisfied. 10 is on the outside and represents completely satisfied. Do this scoring quickly.

The most important thing is to recognise that this isn't about balancing all areas of your life equally. We don't believe that it's possible to have 10 in every area of life at the same time.

Once you have your scores, write down what would make each area a 10. Then score each area in order of importance to you, right now, and write down an approximate percentage of your time that you are currently spending on each area. This should make you very conscious of how you are currently spending your time and allow you to see if this is how you want it to be. It gives you a starting point to change things. This exercise can be a life changer! You will find the full version of this exercise at www .be-more-kid.com.

MOTIVATION: THE FLIP SIDE TO PROCRASTINATION

If we have a coin with procrastination on one side, the flip side is motivation. But motivation can be a double-edged sword. The problem is that most people in life know what they don't want, so their motivation stems from moving away from an outcome. This 'away from motivation' will only kick in when something becomes painful enough that you want to move away from it. In other words, you're moving away from something that you don't want to happen.

What you need to do is change how you're motivated, so that you have a 'towards motivation'. This means you're motivated by the goal or the outcome. It's big, it's bright and when you think about that goal or outcome, it really sets you on fire!

The way to achieve this 'towards motivation' is to address the negative emotions. These are the root cause of that negativity and the way to deal with them is to get rid of your fear and guilt, and find clarity about what you do want in life.

LIFE IS A JOURNEY, NOT A DESTINATION

Where you have to be careful with motivation is ensuring you always have the next thing to move towards. Most people don't have a goal beyond that first goal. They get to that outcome and then they can stall. It's because they're thinking of life as a destination, rather than as a journey.

Kids take life as a journey. It's the way it is, it's fun and one day feels like five years to a kid. But at some point we lose that and all of a sudden it becomes a race to a destination, whether that's utopia, happiness, being the perfect parent, or whatever. People don't have goals beyond their goals. They don't have a notion of what the longer game is. They treat each part of life like a sprint, rather than seeing the whole thing as a marathon.

That's why people often procrastinate, because they only get their backsides in gear when the 'away from' gets big enough to motivate them. But this is the wrong kind of motivation. It is fine to get someone moving, but what they need is a lasting, constant motivation which stops them from procrastinating. That comes from a plan which gives them contentment and hooks them into the pleasures in life.

The other problem with focusing on a destination is that people often don't know what they want, even if they can tell you very clearly what they *don't* want. In this situation it's easy for people to change their plans and make a complete U-turn. They'll start something and won't see it through. And then they'll start doing something completely different. They keep doing this throughout their lives.

The reason they're constantly switching is because they think they're not on the right path. But what if they continued on that path to see where it would take them? The answer is they'd learn an awful lot of things along the way and develop resources and life skills for the future.

Think of it this way: if you get into a car and just start to drive, you're not going to get anywhere. You're just going to drive around aimlessly. You need to know where you're heading, you need a map, you need a plan and you need a route. If you want to take a detour on the drive you can. But there isn't any point in just aimlessly driving around because you don't know when you've 'arrived'.

Now Your Turn: Knowing your own convincer

Knowing whether you are on the right path is important. Knowing your own convincer helps you to understand yourself and your internal motivators better. It also identifies what could currently be causing you uncertainty and even anxiety. We all have an internal convincer, so we'd like you to ask yourself:

How many times, or over what period of time, do you need to do or see something happening, in order to be convinced it's going well?

It might be dependent on the number of times you do or see something, or the period of time you do it for. That doesn't really matter, but what's important is knowing that number or period of time. Without knowing what you need to do or see, it's easy to get so far with something and then not be convinced that it's going well. That's when you'll make another U-turn, without seeing something through to its conclusion. You will find the full version of this exercise at www.be-more-kid.com.

EXCUSES FOR PROCRASTINATION

Many people make excuses for procrastinating. There are several that we come across time and again.

1 **Fate.**

One of the ways people resolve procrastination without doing anything themselves is to say things like, 'It wasn't meant to be', or 'The universe hasn't decided it's for me', or 'I'm not vibrating at the right frequency at the moment'. It's all rubbish. All this does is give them permission to continue to procrastinate or to just give up. Saying, 'I'll leave it up to fate', is in itself a form of procrastination.

This new religion of 'The Universe' is no different to believing God will look after you. It causes people to procrastinate, to avoid taking action and being responsible for themselves, and it gives them an excuse. It becomes self-fulfilling. In most cases they don't do anything, or certainly not what it takes.

But by believing that it wasn't meant to be, they've given themselves permission to do nothing. You always have to start with the destination in mind. Set yourself clear goals around a task and do some work on visualising the end result.

2   **There's not enough time.**

This is a genuine reason people don't achieve what they want, but it doesn't have to be an excuse. Time is the same for everyone; there are 24 hours in a day. The issue isn't that they're not managing time – no one is managing time – it's that they're not managing their tasks within that time.

Time will carry on, no matter what you do, so you need to place your focus on task management. A woman once told us that she didn't have the time to do her marketing and her training. So we asked, 'Who does your shopping?' Her response was, 'I do, I go to the shops twice a week.' We talked about how long it takes, including driving there and back, and compared it to how long it would take to do the shopping online. We went through various aspects of her life like this and by the end of it we'd saved her 10 hours, which was plenty of time to do her marketing.

The issue is that most people don't value their time. What happens is that they expand their tasks to fill the available time, rather than actually managing the tasks themselves. It comes back to the concept of busyness. People will always tell you how busy they are. They're not. They're just busying themselves with tasks that actually aren't important and just run down the clock so that they haven't got time for the tasks they're procrastinating over.

3   **Lack of energy or tiredness.**

This is something a lot of people suffer from. They feel lethargic and can't summon up the energy to deal with what they perceive as difficult tasks. This requires more of a physical, practical resolution. One of the most important things is to get enough sleep.

Sleep is really important for your body and your mind. You need to make sure that you're getting enough sleep for you, and everyone is different; so where one person might need seven hours a night, another might need nine.

But it's not just the amount of sleep that's important, it's also the quality of that sleep. Turn your phone off in the bedroom. Install a blackout blind. Don't have a TV in the bedroom. Your bedroom should be for sex and sleeping, that's it. If you struggle to sleep because you're trying to remember things for the next day, keep a notebook by your bed, write down everything you need to remember for the morning and then allow your brain to forget about it so you can sleep.

Exercise is also important. People often use the excuse that they don't have time to exercise but it should be the other way around: we haven't got time not to exercise, because everything is improved by exercise and sleep. If you get enough sleep and do enough exercise, you'll find you have more quality hours in your day where you feel like you can achieve things.

Diet is another thing that affects our energy levels. We need to eat a well-balanced diet, but many people eat too much sugar and too many carbohydrates. This has the effect of making them sluggish and tired. That means they won't do something.

They won't cook proper food and instead they'll eat snacks, which just puts them into a cycle of feeling worse. It's not just about what you eat either. Eating at the wrong times of day can have a negative impact. And often because their lives are out of control, that's exactly what they do.

Eating a big meal or really sugary stuff late at night affects what happens to your body. When it should be resting and producing hormones to help with all kinds of things, it's busy digesting, so you lose out on all the good stuff.

Water is often really overlooked too. Most people don't drink enough water and as a result are dehydrated and suffer from headaches. They pop pills when they'd be much better off drinking two litres of water throughout the day.

Mark's story

Some years ago I had an arthroscopy on my knee. At the hospital, everything was fine, but a couple of weeks later I stopped sleeping properly. I started having disrupted sleep and then I started aching and sweating. I felt like I had some sort of virus. I just went downhill.

To cut a long story short, they diagnosed me with Chronic Fatigue Syndrome several months later. The doctors told me there was a reasonable chance I'd end up in a wheelchair and that if I got depressed then I'd need to take antidepressants for the rest of my life.

I went to a private consultant and had every blood test known to man. I remember sitting in the consultant's office and he said, 'I know you're looking at me thinking, "Doc, please make me better", but I can't. We don't know what's wrong with you. We can only diagnose you because you've got the symptoms associated with chronic fatigue. You just have to accept that you've got this'. This is a common issue that people who are diagnosed with chronic fatigue or fibromyalgia have.

I knew that my big issue was sleep, so I did a lot of research on sleep. I tried everything: lavender under the pillow, acupuncture, Chinese herbal medicine, I even looked at colonic irrigation because someone told me that might help. In the end what made me start sleeping again was a homeopath. I know that might be a bit controversial. But they gave me some homeopathic pills and I started sleeping again. This helped, but it actually wasn't what made me truly well again.

I think the real cause of my disrupted sleep was that I hadn't dealt with all my sh*tuff over the years. I was full of hurt and sadness and I hadn't dealt with those negative emotions. When I learned strategies professionally in 2009 for letting go of anger, sadness, fear, guilt, hurt and the conflict inside me, that's when I became truly well.

This is a problem a lot of people face. It's what causes their procrastination and overthinking. The root cause is that most people aren't taught how to deal with their emotions. Emotions are what separate us from the rest of

(continued)

the animal kingdom, because they stimulate response, but we don't utilise them in the way they should be.

Being human doesn't just mean you have these emotions, it also means you can control them. You need to release them and deal with them in an adult way. You want a strategy to be able to be resilient to life and let go of this *sh*tuff*.

THERE IS NO MAGIC WAND

The mistake too many people make is looking for someone to wave a magic wand and do everything for them. We're sorry to disappoint you, but there is no magic wand. If you're reading this, you have to want to make these changes. We can give you all the suggestions in the world but they won't make a blind bit of difference if you don't do something. You have to do it, you have to want to do it and you have to make the time to do it.

This is a do-with process, not a do-to process. What we mean by that is that we can give you tools that you can use, but we can't do things for you. We'll open the door but you still have to walk through it, we're not able to carry you, nor would we want to.

We're not saying that you'll read this book and life will suddenly become simple. What we are giving you is new ways of thinking and some tools you can use to make active changes in your life. But if you have no intention of actually going through the exercises and putting active changes into your life, nothing will change. This is a book about doing things and you have to play your part as well. We guarantee that by doing nothing, nothing will change, but if you follow what we recommend and complete the exercises, who knows what you will achieve?

BE MORE KID

When we're children, emotion just comes out. We stamp our feet, we cry, we shout, whatever it might be. We're not saying that adults should have tantrums to deal with their negative emotions. What we're saying is that you had fantastic resources as a child and you still have access to those, so all you need to do is tap into those resources and combine them with the lessons that you've learned from being an adult. You're utilising the best part of being an adult with the resources that we had as a child, which is a winning combination!

You have to look to the spontaneity of children. Look at how they do things that they enjoy and aim to achieve that same joy that you see in children. They think about what would bring them the most joy right now and that's what they want to do. There's a lot of power in that and it can be incredibly motivating.

Obviously we have the constraints of an adult world, but when was the last time you asked yourself, 'What do I really want to do right now?' and gave yourself permission to actually do it? Whether it's reading a book, going for a walk or even skipping down the street. We shouldn't put barriers up but instead should trust ourselves, pay attention to what we actually want to do and just do it.

Prioritise and do the things that are important to you because experience and enjoyment is everything. That's what we look back on, not whether we ironed all the socks and underwear. Lots of adults have great intentions but never do anything. Intentions do not equal results.

You've got to dream big. Remember the limitless possibilities from childhood, remember the curiosity you had for the world around you. Reconnect with that simplistic, 'dream big' joy of life that kids have. Think about the things that you enjoyed doing when you were growing up. Reconnect with things you're passionate about, that are fun and that give you fulfilment in your life.

What instrument did you play as a kid? What sport did you play as a kid? What was your favourite film when you were growing up? If you pick up that instrument, go back to that sport or spend an afternoon watching that film, you'll feel amazing. Be like a kid, just get on with it and do it ... and enjoy it!

CHAPTER 4

PASSENGER OR DRIVER?

Being the driver in your life is all about taking control. If you're the passenger in your life there are no results. You just drift along and go where the driver takes you. There appear to be no options, but that couldn't be further from the truth.

LIVING IN THE GREY ZONE

Most people live in what we call the Grey Zone – remember this from Chapter 1? This is a place that people settle into, it's their comfort zone. It's a place where life isn't too bad, but it's not great either. They might moan about wanting a bit more money, or having a few more holidays, but they aren't prepared to take responsibility to make those things happen. They like not having that responsibility. It's mundane. Often the only time they get out of this Grey Zone is when they book a holiday.

Sometimes people go the other way. Something bad happens in their life and, bit by bit, they pick themselves up and go from that really bad experience or time back to the Grey Zone, where they settle in and stop again.

But the trouble with the Grey Zone is that people mistake it for something it's not. They think they have freedom there, but they're not taking control of their lives so this isn't real freedom. That causes conflict and in turn can lead to mental health issues.

WHY WE STAY TRAPPED IN THE GREY ZONE

The Grey Zone is secure. It's where people spend most of their lives. There are pockets of time when they see outside the Grey Zone and know there's something more, but because the Grey Zone feels safe and comfortable and they've got so used to being a passenger in their life, they don't know how to break out of it.

One of the reasons this happens is because the world wants you to be a passenger. You're conditioned throughout your life to take the path of least resistance. When you receive bad news, everyone tells you to slow down and take your time. If you fail at something, the response will often be, 'At least you tried'. It's very rare that someone will say, 'No, don't accept that. Sort yourself out and do it again'.

When a child takes its first step and falls over, we applaud that step and ignore the fall, encouraging them to take further steps knowing that they will probably fall again. Yet when adults fall, we bring it to their attention. It's called failure and people around you attempt to make you feel better about failing, or take pride in telling you that they knew it wouldn't work. This makes it feel okay to be a passenger and encourages people to stay in the Grey Zone.

Another reason people stay trapped in the Grey Zone is that they can't comprehend what's outside of it because they have no neural networks to connect with. When we talk about neural networks, we mean mental processes. They're so entrenched in the Grey Zone that they can't see anything else.

They won't perceive that they're in the Grey Zone any more than they'll perceive something beyond it. People need guidance to develop the thought processes and experience they need to lift themselves out of the Grey Zone.

But becoming a driver isn't a popular choice either. Tallest Poppy Syndrome describes how people who have achieved high status are often cut down, criticised or resented. It comes from the idea that you want a uniform field of poppies, and you cut down any that grow too tall because they stand out from the rest.

When you become a driver, you stand out. This makes other people realise how miserable their lives are. Rather than ask how they can improve their lives, their reaction is to fight against it. They try to bring you back to their level instead of rising up to join you.

WHY DO WE BECOME A PASSENGER?

All of these things keep people trapped in the Grey Zone and ensure they remain a passenger in their lives. But why do you become a passenger in the first place? There are a number of triggers that cause you to climb out of the driving seat and take your place as a passenger.

Overwhelmed – feeling overwhelmed by everything happening in your life, particularly when you're going through a difficult patch, is a common reason to become a passenger. People feel as though there's nothing they can do about the situation they're in and they give up control.

Believing their own excuses – people are great at finding reasons not to do things. They'll have lots of reasons and excuses that they can't do something, but they'll believe that these reasons give them no option but to stay on their current course. They'll use excuses like, 'I'm too old', or 'I'm too young', or 'I have kids and I don't have childcare'.

Blaming others – people are very quick to blame others for the situations they find themselves in. They blame their parents and their childhood. When things go wrong people are even more likely to look for an outside cause to blame for their problems. When you blame others for things that go wrong you stop looking inside yourself to find out what you can learn. When you put control outside yourself there's no opportunity to learn and that's when you become a passenger.

Don't want responsibility – people will often say they want a new job, more money, more holidays and so on, but they're not prepared to do what it takes to get there. They feel conflicted about doing what it takes because they're scared of things going wrong and they don't have faith in their abilities.

This often manifests as buying a lottery ticket, or using affirmations or the law of attraction to manifest the life that they want. The law of attraction is only the first step. It's helpful because it creates a vision of what you want, but all too often people fail to take the actions required to bring this vision to life.

Labels – we're given labels throughout our lives. Many people use these labels as a reason to not do things. They tell themselves it's not their fault that they can't do x, y, z. These labels are disempowering. It's particularly apparent in people who are diagnosed with a health condition.

As soon as they're told their diagnosis, it becomes a reason not to do things. And yet we've all heard stories about people achieving amazing things through great adversity. The difference is that the people who achieve these great things don't use their label as an excuse to become a passenger.

Relying on support – people are conditioned to look for support. If you have a hard time, you're told to rely on others and get support in your life. When people fall ill, they're often referred to a support group. These groups can help initially, but because everyone in that group is having the same problem, they can't offer real assistance to one another to help each other get better. Another potential issue arises when people become affiliated with a group because they share the same problem, but then they get better. All of a sudden, they're no longer part of that group and if they've come to feel like they belong there due to this shared identity, it can hinder their recovery.

HOW TO TELL IF YOU'RE A PASSENGER IN YOUR LIFE

One of the most obvious signs that you're a passenger rather than a driver in your life is if you frequently use phrases like, 'I can't do that', or 'It's ok for you, but I can't do that'. Passengers will always have excuses for why they can't do something.

Another sign of being a passenger is making other people the cause of your emotions and feelings. Saying things like, 'They make me so angry', or 'He makes me so sad', puts someone else in charge of your emotions. You're giving away control and failing to recognise that you have the power to change things.

Looking for someone else to complete you is another sign that you're a passenger in your life. People put a lot of emphasis on 'finding their other half', which implies that on their own they're not enough. They're looking for another person with the qualities they believe they're lacking themselves.

Parents will often live through their children. They'll put all their focus on their children achieving certain things rather than doing those things themselves. This is different to supporting your children while you're still doing things for yourself. As a passenger you're sidelining yourself, rather than continuing to be the driver of your life while supporting your children to do the same.

Labels are one of the reasons people become passengers, but if you find you're constantly using a label to justify not doing something, that's another sign that you've become a passenger.

Looking for escapism from your life is an indication that you're a passenger. That escapism might come through alcohol, drugs, TV shows, holidays or many other forms. Feeling like you need to escape in the first place is a sign you're not in the driving seat.

Recognising that you're a passenger is the first step. The second step is learning how to put yourself back in the driving seat.

Ed's story

A few short years ago, I felt like my life was falling apart. It was as though I'd knocked one spinning plate into the next and now everything was coming crashing down. My relationship of 19 years had broken down. I was facing bankruptcy and an investigation due to fraud by a co-director. Everything was going wrong. Looking at that big picture was overwhelming and scary and there didn't seem to be any way out.

I didn't feel as though I had any control. I was ready to sit back and let everything fall down around me. Ride out the storm, so to speak, and see if there were any pieces to pick up at the end. But then I decided to implement a concept I'd learned from Mark and Nicky a few years ago ... 'cause and effect'. Was I going to accept the effects of what was happening in my life, or was I going to operate 'at cause' and take back some control?

I needed to get back into the position of being a driver in my life, not an unwitting passenger who kept closing their eyes to block out the road in front of them. I embraced the concept. I started to take action. The great thing was, even the smallest action felt like a significant achievement. It showed me that I did have control after all. It gave me the confidence to tackle another thing, then another, then another. The feeling of succeeding was addictive. Before I knew it, I had both hands on the wheel and was firmly in control of the direction my life was taking.

HOW TO BECOME A DRIVER

When you're living in the Grey Zone, you're living life unconsciously. What we mean by that is you're living on autopilot and not making any real choices. This is how many people live 95% of the time. They just react to events in a stimulus–response way, like Pavlov's dog. There is a difference between reacting to events and having the ability to respond. When you react, your actions are dictated by unconscious beliefs, values, conflicts and previous experiences that are part of your programming. It's often as if someone or something takes over and you are the observer of your own life.

The first step towards becoming a driver is to be consciously aware and start living your life consciously. You need to break out of your automatic programming and make conscious choices in your life.

Start by imagining that you're coming towards the end of your life. Maybe you're 90 years old, maybe you're 120. What will you care about when you're reviewing your life? Will you look back and realise that all the excuses you gave stopped you living the life you wanted? Will you regret not taking chances? Will you wish that you'd put fewer limits on yourself?

The great thing is you're not 90, or 120 (and if you are it's never too late to start a new life), so how can you make sure that when you look back you don't have regrets? Whenever you find yourself giving an excuse as to why you can't do something, flip it on its head. Ask instead what you can do to get around that issue and make something happen. Instead of saying, 'I can't go on that course because I don't have childcare', say 'Where can I find childcare so that I can go on that course?'

Listen to kids. They don't take 'No' for an answer. If they want to do something, they find a way.

Asking that positive question puts you back on course. It stops you focusing on what you don't have and makes you focus on finding solutions. Once you flip one thing like that, look at other aspects of your life and think, 'What else can I flip?' Embrace the mindset of, 'How can I be the driver of this?'

Another powerful approach is to avoid using the word 'try'. It presupposes failure and gives the wrong kind of signal to your unconscious mind. Your unconscious mind will always give you what you ask it for. As soon as you 'try' to do something, all you'll get is an excuse not to be successful. As the great philosopher Yoda says, 'Do or do not, there is no try'.

Don't stop until you become the driver. Adults have a habit of asking for something once and if they don't get it then they feel embarrassed to ask again. Children don't have this. When they know what they want, they pursue something until they get it or until they get a definitive 'no', and even then they'll still keep asking!

Ed's story

My daughter Jaime has given me a perfect example of being a tenacious driver! I told her that once I wiped my old phone, I'd let her have it. As with life, one thing leads to another and it wasn't at the top of my priority list. It was, however, at the top of hers and every other day for more than two weeks she asked me when I was going to wipe it and when she could have it! She wasn't embarrassed, she was persistent and it paid off as I finally did it.

You have to stay strong when you're becoming a driver. As we've said, the world encourages you to be a passenger so it will take strength and resolve to stand up to that and make active choices that put you in the driving seat of your life.

DON'T LET YOUR LIFE BE DEFINED

Nicky's story

Less than 30 seconds. That's all it took to bring 25 years of hard work to an abrupt end. Friends told me, 'You must feel so angry', and wanted me to blame the driver. Doctors told me how anxious I must be feeling.

But I didn't feel angry or anxious, I didn't even feel sad and I certainly didn't blame anyone. People told me that it wasn't normal to think this way about a traumatic 'accident'.

It was entirely my choice to be where I was at 7.47 a.m. on that Monday morning in February 2010. To be where I was at that precise moment when the red van pulled out of the junction and accelerated into the back of our car. And it was certainly my choice to be leaning forward, seat belt still on, at that exact moment to collect my bag off the floor so I could make a quick exit when we arrived at the railway station.

As the van hit us, my head was thrown backwards hitting the headrest hard and I felt a searing pain in my head and neck. I was totally dazed, but I remember saying to myself in the ambulance on the way to the hospital that, overall, I was okay.

I knew something had changed when I was struggling to negotiate my way around the trolleys in the hospital corridor, and then not being able to fit boxes of food items into the shopping basket. How strange. I knew what I wanted to do, but I couldn't seem to do it.

What followed over the coming days and weeks was even more bizarre. I realised that I had forgotten lots of everyday words, which made speaking to anyone really challenging; sometimes I couldn't even work out what language someone was speaking, even though Mark assured me it was my native language of English.

It became evident that I had lost my perception of speed and distance when I stepped out into the road and narrowly missed being hit by a car, thinking the car to be farther away than it actually was. After looking to the

(continued)

right and forgetting to look left when crossing the road the following day, it became clear that I wasn't safe to be out on my own and of course driving was also impossible.

I had been transformed from someone who was totally independent, flying around the UK on a weekly basis for work, into someone who couldn't even leave the house on their own.

After cutting myself whilst preparing food and being surrounded by thousands of shards of smashed glass through misjudging the distance to the cupboard whilst putting away a wine glass, badly gashing my wrist, it became apparent that being in the kitchen was also something that I could no longer do. What on earth was wrong with me?

Every morning I woke up with the belief that when I opened my eyes everything would be back to normal, but that didn't happen.

The left side of my face was numb, as was my left arm, and I dragged my left leg when I walked. I was no longer able to take part in the sports that I loved and in the months after the accident I put on 2½ stone in weight. I wasn't recognisable as the person I used to be, yet I was determined that I would get my life back.

In November 2010, after being off work for nine months, I told my consultants and GP that I wanted to go back to work. I believed that I could re-programme my mind and strengthen my body, and returning to work would be the way that I would do that.

Over the months, I had created new strategies that helped me through each day; for example, planning in advance and writing down the answers to any questions I might be asked. These were everyday questions that a five-year-old would be able to answer, like my date of birth, my address and my phone number, so I could simply read them out if asked.

I created a plan for a gradual return to work, one morning the first week, two mornings the second, three mornings the third, increasing to full time. What hadn't occurred to me was that by returning to work my employers quite rightly would think I was well enough to be there, whereas in fact I wasn't.

But being back in the workplace put me under tremendous strain as I couldn't plan for what I would be asked and I got strange looks when my reply to easy questions was that I simply didn't know.

As part of my rehabilitation, I insisted on catching the train on my own. By the time I had struggled to work out the ticket machine, fathomed what the electronic displays were telling me (on more than one occasion catching the wrong train and having to find my way back) and walked the short distance to the office, I was totally exhausted.

On my first day back at work I couldn't remember how to turn on my computer and had to ask my manager to do it for me. The office was really noisy; after the accident I had developed an inability to hear what someone was saying when there was background noise, so I had learned to lip-read as much as I could and I guessed the rest. My employer was incredibly supportive, yet they struggled to find me work that I was able to do.

I never made it back to full time and eventually was dismissed from work on the grounds of capability.

Less than 30 seconds was all it took to bring 25 years of hard work to an abrupt end. I had been promoted twice in the previous three years and I knew where I was going and what I wanted to achieve … and there it was, all over.

… Yet, it wasn't all over. This was just the beginning. An enormous opportunity lay in front of me to use everything that I knew to return to full health both mentally and physically, and not only for my own benefit, but also to use this life-changing experience to help others change their lives too, whatever their starting point.

Rather than accepting what had happened and was happening in my body and mind, I started looking at what I needed to do to change the way things were happening. I hired a personal trainer to help build up my strength. I changed my diet. I used the work I was doing through NLP to help change my thought processes and my life. So I am actually the best advert for what we do as NLP Master Trainers.

And here I am, nearly a decade later, telling the story of how I turned things around and made sure I was still the driver in my life.

Ed's story

My uncle John is 80 years old at the time of writing. At 75, he was diagnosed with Parkinson's disease. He's always been very fit. He would climb mountains and walk a lot. When most people are diagnosed with a condition like Parkinson's they stop doing the things they've always done. Not my Uncle John. Since being diagnosed, he's been climbing and hiking more. The hills and mountains he's hiking up aren't as big as the ones he's climbed in the past, but he still hikes almost every day.

The NHS have even asked him to go and speak to small groups of people who have also been diagnosed with Parkinson's to show them that the diagnosis doesn't mean you have to just stop. His doctors are amazed at his strength, mobility and skillset. He's got the attitude that he's not going to be defined by a label and that's so powerful. It's why he's still able to lead a really healthy, active and happy life.

ESCAPING THE GREY ZONE IS DIFFERENT FOR EVERYONE

Everyone's Grey Zone will be different. Just because someone seems successful to the outside world doesn't mean they haven't become a passenger in their own life.

We recently met a man who, to outside appearances, was really successful. He used to run an audiovisual company and worked at big venues like the NEC in Birmingham. The company was doing really well. But other companies started to come in and undercut his prices. He was having to travel to London all the time and be away from his family, and he felt like he was stuck in the rat race.

Now he runs a small alpaca farm. He realised that running a busy and successful business like that wasn't what he wanted from his life. So he sold his business, bought the alpaca farm and made a complete change to his life. He recognised that he was missing out on seeing his kids grow up. He wanted to have a life that made him feel good and that allowed him to give something back.

What he does is hard work, but it's all on his terms. He wouldn't change it for the world, and he gets to spend plenty of time with his family. It would have been really easy for him to think about selling his business, but still carry on with it. He could have said that he couldn't give up the audiovisual business because he needed the money, or had to pay a mortgage, but he didn't. He took a leap of faith and made sure he was the driver in his life.

Another example of escaping the Grey Zone comes from a couple we met some years ago. They'd been on holiday to Spain, doing what many people do to escape their Grey Zone, when they decided that they wanted to have a life like that all the time. They came back from their holiday, sold their house, liquidated all their assets in the UK, gave up their jobs and bought a small place in Spain outright.

They had some money in their pockets, but no sustainable income, but they just knew that if they didn't take the plunge then, that they'd be stuck in the mundane, 9–5, Monday–Friday life forever. For six months of the year they live in their place in Spain and to make money they do odd jobs, like picking people up from the airport or looking after other people's properties while they're away. They get to enjoy the nice weather and live in a place they love. But then from October to March they go travelling.

What we should add here is that we are not promoting spontaneously giving up your job. We are very much in favour of planning major changes such as this and we will come onto this a little later.

BE MORE KID

One of the biggest mistakes adults make is to let life drive them rather than them driving life. It paralyses them and means they remain a passenger rather than taking control and becoming a driver. Kids tend not to think things through. They don't get caught up in how much effort it's going to take to reach the end goal, they just focus on the next step. It's amazing how, once you take that first step, the step after that becomes obvious.

Before you know it, you've taken a journey and it's led you somewhere amazing. But it all starts with that first step. Kids will take that leap of faith

easily. Adults teeter on the edge. They use excuses. There's always a reason not
to do something. Kids don't have that.

Kids are also much better at not letting labels define them than adults are.
Children with medical problems often have enormous strength of character.
They don't have self-pity, they don't get caught up in the ideas of 'I can't' or 'I
shouldn't'; they just do it. As adults we need to learn from this and put it to
work in our own lives.

Josh is a teenager who embodies everything we've talked about. At the
age of five he was diagnosed with leukaemia and spent the next three years
in and out of hospitals. He's cured now, but in Ed's role as a radio presenter
with Heart, he did the Three Peaks with Josh during the annual challenge for
Global's Make Some Noise charity. In three days, they climbed the UK's three
highest peaks.

Ed's story

It was quite hard work. We didn't get much sleep, it was windy, it rained. But
it was Josh who kept us going. Not because of what he said, but because of
how he behaved. He didn't moan once. And whenever you started thinking
about how hard it was, or how tired you were, or how horrible the weather
was, you realised that you were walking alongside someone who'd beaten
leukaemia and had such a fantastic attitude. Ten years ago he was in a hospital, now he's up a mountain. He's all about what he can do and he won't
allow anything to stop him.

He now runs a charity that he set up with his mum to support other kids
going through what he did. He does this to tell them not to be defined by
what they've been told. And he shows them, because he does more now
than you'd expect.

Ask yourself now, what seat are you in? Are you the driver or are you a passenger? If you're the passenger then there's something you need to do.

PART II

REDISCOVERING YOU

In the first part of the book we've looked at why we could all benefit from being more kid. The whole concept centres around taking yourself back to how it felt and what your state of mind was when you were a child. It's about finding that feeling of hope and possibility, of dreaming big and feeling free, rather than burdened or constrained.

When you're a kid, you have exponential possibilities. You're amazing and there's nothing you can't do. If you look back at what you learned as a child, you'll realise you smashed every goal. Learning to walk and talk are things you take for granted now, but they were huge things to master. And you succeeded.

Kids are often happy for no particular reason. They're awe-some, meaning they're full of awe and wonder at the world around them. They're not afraid to ask why, which is something that gets beaten out of us as we become adults.

Young children take information at face value and don't try to fit it into a box. They don't need closure or certainty. One of the biggest things is that they don't mind failure. If something doesn't work, they'll just try something else. They don't dwell on failure. They have a joy and bliss from living in the moment and just being.

But as you get older you lose sight of your achievements and how amazing you truly are. You worry about failing and you look for certainty at every turn.

You're exposed to environmental conditions that put restrictions on you. For many children, going to school or nursery is when they start consciously reasoning things and lose touch with their unconscious mind. They're taught a certain way of behaving and greater emphasis is placed on conforming to society's expectations.

We're not suggesting that you relive your childhood, or that everyone had a delightful childhood. We know that's not the case and that some people have experienced very troubled childhoods.

What this part – and indeed this whole book – is about is blending the intelligence of an adult with the freedom of a child. We want to help you tap back into that simplicity of childhood that's present when you're very young.

In this second part of the book we're going to help you reconnect with some of the resources you may have lost touch with and remind you of how you can tap into them now you're an adult.

CHAPTER 5

IF YOU DON'T LIKE IT, DON'T DO IT

A s you grow up, you're taught the rules of the game of life. Social conformity is a big thing and many people become people-pleasers. You're taught values that are very sacrificial, in that if you sacrifice yourself now, you'll get a reward later.

Often you give up the things you enjoy in order to please others. You say yes to a lot of things you don't want to do. You lose the ability to say, 'No, actually, I don't want to do that'. Internally people treat it like a bartering system. They tell themselves, 'Now I've done that, I can expect them to do the same thing for me in the future'.

This creates an expectation and when the other person doesn't offer to reciprocate, you get angry; with the potential for delivering all the dis-ease, conflict and stress we talked about in Part I.

People fill their lives with things they really don't want to do and people they don't want to see out of politeness or a sense of guilt. They then get themselves in a position where they don't know how to say no. And they worry that saying no will cause someone to take offence. Whenever they do say no to something, they often have to make up an elaborate story or excuse, or even feign illness, rather than just saying no.

One of the problems is that they don't let go of the people who don't add value to their lives, or who added value but at a different time. They make plans to go for a drink with Jane, an old school friend they haven't seen for 20 years, out of a sense of obligation, when they'd rather stay at home, have a bath and drink a glass of wine. Jane was probably thinking the same thing!

People stop evaluating the role others play in their lives. They continue friendships out of a sense of politeness, when really the relationship no longer serves either of you.

Kids don't do this. They only have friends who add value to their lives. Sometimes that can be a bit callous in that they make friends with the person who has the computer or the phone. But the point is that they're always looking for someone that adds value to their lives. Do you?

THE POWER OF SAYING NO

There's a lot of power in saying no to things and not explaining or giving reasons why. People clog up their lives with things they don't want to do and then they don't have time for the things they care about.

When you say yes to things out of a sense of obligation, all you're doing is stopping yourself doing the things you really want to do. You don't have time to do the things you'll enjoy, spend time with the people you want to see or just have fun, because you're doing all these things you don't actually want to.

Now Your Turn: The power of 'No'

Make a list of all the things you say yes to in your life that you wish you didn't.

For one week, only say yes to the things you want to do. If you don't want to do something, say no. Don't feel obliged to give an explanation, just say no and leave it at that. See how much more time you have for the things you want to do. You will find the full version of this exercise at www .be-more-kid.com.

BEING AUTHENTIC

Kids say things like they are. They state the obvious, sometimes to the point as a parent where you're embarrassed at what they come out with. But they don't mean any offence, they're just being honest and authentic. Out of the mouths of babes, as the saying goes.

There's a lot of power in going through your life being authentic to who you are and being open and honest. It also means the people around you know who you are and what you stand for, and that means they know where they stand as well.

It's what happens in groups of young kids. Everybody knows what everyone's like because they're all honest and authentic.

Ed's story

My son Jack likes to wear certain brands of clothing. I went to the shops just before his birthday and bought him a nice hoodie. I thought it was the kind of brand he liked and I spent quite a bit of money on it.

When I gave it to him I did something that most of us do. I said, 'Look, if you don't like it, just say and we can change it, it's no problem'. When he opened it, he said 'Dad, I don't like it. Do you think we could change it and go to the shop so I could choose one I like?'

I felt crushed. But then I realised that actually he's got to wear this all the time. Why would I want him to wear something he doesn't like? Why would he feel he has to wear something he doesn't like just to please me? He's done absolutely the right thing. It's his gift and he should choose if he wants it or not, otherwise there's no point in it being a gift.

Jack didn't overthink it. And I think it was a great way of handling it. Most people wouldn't do that. They'd say thank you, smile and then never wear the thing.

Think about how behaving like that would transform a workplace, a friendship group or a family. If people adopted that attitude there'd be no backstabbing, no sniping and no trying to guess if someone is being honest with you. It would force you to accept people for who they are, because you're being who you are.

As adults, if we all agreed to play by the same rules, just think how much simpler our lives would be.

This all ties into the idea of honesty and self-acceptance. People have a tendency to think of things externally. They say things like, 'If only this wasn't happening', or 'If this happened then I'd be happy'. But really what they need to do is accept who they are and where they are in life.

Not having this self-acceptance creates conflict. That leads to everything we talked about in Part I: stress, dis-ease within the body and general unhappiness.

People try to achieve this sense of feeling okay within themselves. They're looking for okay-ness rather than looking at how they can be authentic within themselves. They've got so much going on and are so worried about fear, hurt and rejection they're not okay.

The cultural norms, values and behaviours that we're conditioned to as children remain with us as adults and it's a kind of environmental pollution. Because we're so cloaked in this 'pollution' we struggle to be honest. We need to move away from this idea of okay-ness and clear up our own *sh*tuff* so that we can be authentic again.

Look at kids. They don't worry about the implications of their actions. If they want to run around like an aeroplane they just do it, they're not held back by worrying that everyone else in the room will think they're stupid. They just do whatever's important to them at that moment in time.

RETAINING YOUR STRUCTURE

Although the title of this chapter is 'If you don't like it, don't do it', we're not suggesting that you just stop doing all the things you don't like straight away.

If you don't like going to work, you shouldn't just leave your job tomorrow, for instance, that needs a plan!

We all have to do tasks that we don't like sometimes. It might be filing our tax return, it might be doing admin at work; there are some jobs you just have to do. The key is in understanding how these menial tasks fit into your higher purpose. It might be that you run a business that you love, so to keep that going there are certain admin jobs you need to do even if you don't like them.

The way you have to approach these tasks is by framing them within the context of your higher purpose. We can then get motivated to do those tasks, as there is now a good reason to do them.

In fact, we need routine and structure. If you look at a kid's life, they have a lot of structure. There are things that they have to do that they don't like. That might be going to bed early or cleaning their teeth. This chapter isn't about the things you have to do within your general structure, but about the over and above things we do.

ESCAPING THE TRAP OF UNFULFILLMENT

If you really detest going to work, look at how you can restructure your life to make that 'must-do' more enjoyable. Make a plan to change your job to something you're passionate about.

Evaluate all the excuses you make for not changing this part of your life. Are they financial? Is it the mortgage, school fees, the desire to have regular family holidays that's preventing you from taking action? Ask yourself how much of that brings you long-term joy.

Remember the RAS (reticular activating system) in Part I? Your brain is trained to seek out similarity and familiarity. If you focus on all the reasons why you can't do something, you won't. What you need to do is flip the situation and find ways around all of your excuses. Make a mental commitment to a course of action and you'll find a solution.

Now Your Turn: What's stopping you?

Make a list of all the things you want to do in your life, yet for whatever reason you haven't done them.

Next List all the reasons you can't do each of those things. Then make a list of all the reasons you could do them and how you can get around the obstacles you've identified. Think about which obstacles are actually real and which are just accepted without question.

Be honest and get to the real reasons you are not doing the things that you want to! Asking yourself the question, 'How can I make this happen?' is a game changer. You will find the full version of this exercise at www.be-more-kid.com.

BE MORE KID

Mark's story

About seven or eight years ago, Nicky and I went to the seaside for a day out. Being big kids, we ended up in the arcade. We won all these tickets – you know the kind of thing where you need about 1,000 to get a glider or something. Anyway, we had enough for two water pistols.

We looked at each other with a glint in our eyes and each ran to the bathroom to fill them up. Then we chased each other around the pier at Weston-super-Mare, squirting each other. We were laughing, it was joyous. I even hid behind this giant, tattoo-covered man to get cover from Nicky squirting me.

But so many of the people around us were looking on with horror and disdain. I think some of it was envy. They were looking at how much fun we were having and trying to remember the last time they had that much fun.

By the end of it we were laughing and had the biggest grins on our faces. It just felt so good.

When was the last time you did something like that? When was the last time you played? When was the last time you lived completely for the moment without a thought for what anyone else was thinking?

At what point did you decide you couldn't do something? Would two kids have run around a pier squirting each other with water pistols? Absolutely. Why can't you?

The problem with adults is that they think too much, and that's what we're going to talk about in the next chapter.

CHAPTER 6

YOU THINK TOO MUCH

We covered overthinking earlier in the book. This chapter is about how we interpret other people's words and assign meaning that isn't there.

Think about how young children interpret what they're told. They will take things as they're intended and often interpret them literally. One of our graduates told us a wonderful story about how challenging it was to wash her children in the shower. Every night they'd be bouncing up and down in the shower, making it really difficult for her to wash them.

She assumed that they really enjoyed having a shower and were just excited. But one day she finally said, 'Can you not just stand still so I can wash you?' Their response was, 'Well, we're just doing what daddy does'. At this point she asked, 'What do you mean?' And they said, 'Well, Dad says he's just going to jump in the shower'.

That's a really good example of what children do. They act on words without applying any meaning to them.

As people get older, they tend to apply meaning to what's being said. The problem in most cases is that this interpretation often has a negative spin. It stops people enjoying things, because they think about all the things that could go wrong and don't just treat things for what they are.

For example, sometimes people will take on other people's problems as though they're their own. There's a tendency to think that because someone is telling you about their problem that they want you to do something about it. But is that really the intention of the person who's shared their problem with you? Often the answer is no.

The interpretation comes from you.

Adults will often think too much about what's been said to them. Their own negative beliefs about themselves start to come into play, as well as what they think of the world and of other people. Too often they go down this route of thinking without stopping to ask, 'What did they actually say? Those words literally mean that. The rest I've put my own meaning to'.

How many times have you read an email and thought, 'Oooh, the tone of that is really harsh?' But here's the thing, an email doesn't have a tone. It's just words on a screen. You're creating the tone and it comes from your interpreta tion of the world, what you think of the person who sent it and so on.

Similarly, how often have you skimmed through an email in a rush and thought it sounded harsh, only to read it again later and realise the email is perfectly fine and doesn't say what you thought it said.

The mood you're in when you read an email can change your interpretation of it. If you read an email in a bad mood as you're about to leave work, you often find that when you're in a better mood the following morning and you look again that it reads completely differently.

What we want you to understand is that it's important to take communica-tion at face value, and not interpret it in any way, except using the facts you have in front of you.

YOUR MODEL OF THE WORLD

To understand why we do this, it may be best if we explain how our brains pro-cess all of the information in the world around us. Research has shown that 11 million bits of sensory information bombard our senses every second. That's a lot of information! It includes everything that's going on around us, what we can see, hear, feel, smell and taste.

In order to process that, we have to take it into our nervous system. We can only take this information through our five senses – visual (sight), auditory (sound), kinaesthetic (touch), olfactory (smell) and gustatory (taste).

But there's still far too much information for our nervous system to process, so we need to cut it down. To do that we delete some of it, generalise other parts and distort the information to enable our nervous system to process it.

During this process of deletion, distortion and generalisation, we filter it using our own model of the world. This model is made up of our filters, such as our values which define what's important to us, and it's from this information that we form our beliefs. These beliefs will cloud how we actually interpret the information inside of us. We always prove ourselves right, don't we?

Another of our filters is our personality traits. These will also affect how we interpret the information we get from the world around us.

So, if one of your personality traits was that you needed someone to tell you that you had done a good job, and feedback wasn't forthcoming, then you either wouldn't move on until you had the feedback or you might think that people don't care about your work. You would delete, distort and generalise the information outside of you to prove you right.

Our attitude will also determine how we filter external information. So, if we have a positive attitude, use positive language and look for opportunities, we're more likely to interpret things in a positive way than if we use negative language and are always looking for the things that we don't want to happen.

All of those things act as filters to help us cut down the vast amount of information that we see outside of us, and they direct our focus. This word 'focus' is really important, because where you direct your focus will determine your behaviour and results. By this point our nervous system has reduced that 11 million bits of information per second to about 126 bits per second, which is our conscious focus. The rest of it is still there, but it goes into our unconscious.

This combination and interaction of your unconscious filters (your values, beliefs, attitudes, language, previous memories and decisions) makes up your unique model of the world. This means that everyone will interpret things differently. What it's important to realise is that you can change your model of the world and therefore change how you interpret things.

Now Your Turn: Exploring your model of the world

Think of a specific situation that isn't going as well for you as you would like. Maybe it's your job or it could be perhaps that you haven't got the relationship that you want. These are just examples, so whatever you choose will be fine as long as it's about you.

Whilst holding this situation in your thoughts, explore the following in your mind:

1. What's important to you about this situation?
2. What previous memories do you have where something similar has happened to this?
3. What emotions do you have about this current situation and what emotions do you have about those past similar memories? Are they the same emotions or different?
4. What decisions are you considering making about this situation and what past situations are you basing your options on?
5. Notice what language you are using in your thoughts about this situation. Is it positive language? Negative language? Something else?

Once you begin exploring your thoughts and what's behind them, you begin to realise the current decisions that we make are entirely based on our own personal model of the world, which includes things such as our personal values, memories, past decisions, beliefs that we hold about ourselves and the world around us, our attitude and our individual personality traits.

If those components of your model of the world are positive and helpful, then they will support you with how you react to situations and how you resolve problems. If they are the opposite, then you will be battling against those each time something comes up for you. You will find the full version of this exercise at www.be-more-kid.com.

HOW YOUR MODEL OF THE WORLD INFLUENCES SELF-TALK

We all have internal self-talk, which is a running commentary of what is happening inside our heads. Some people may call it thinking, which is fine too. Your model of the world will determine your self-talk. Often this can be very negative. This will also influence how you interpret things, how you interact and how you communicate with other people.

It also dictates how you present yourself to the outside world and how you behave. If you have an 'inferential' personality trait, it means you are likely to attribute meaning to something that just isn't there.

For example, how do you respond if someone says to you, 'Where did you get your shoes?' If you interpret that literally, you'll answer with, 'I bought them in XYZ shop', or 'I got them in Vegas', or whatever.

But someone with negative beliefs about themselves and negative self-talk might start thinking, 'They don't like my shoes. They wouldn't be asking that if they liked them. I knew I shouldn't have worn them'.

Someone with positive beliefs about themselves and positive self-talk might interpret that question completely differently and start thinking, 'They must really love my shoes! I bet they're going to buy a pair exactly like mine'.

Although the positive response might seem better, it's not right to attribute meaning in either a positive or negative way. You've been asked a simple question that requires a simple answer. Whether you decide the person asking the question is being complimentary or negative is irrelevant. All you're doing in that situation is assigning meaning that probably isn't there.

This is how situations get confused. You can assume either a good or a bad thing. Then the other person interprets what you've said in the same way and, before you know it, you're both at a completely new place that isn't true for either of you.

The simplest way to find out if you understand what someone is saying to you is to ask them a direct question. Taking the shoes example, you could ask, 'Do you think these shoes go with this coat?' But in doing so, you need to not take offence if the person you're asking gives you their honest answer, which could be 'No'.

BE MORE KID

As people grow from being a child into an adult, many change from being literal to being inferential. They can often stop being themselves due to the complex interactions of the filters that form their model of the world. This often complicates interactions and can lead to people seeing negative or positive in completely neutral situations.

Look at children in a playground. They have a really honest exchange of information because they ask a question and they answer a question. They don't interpret the answers in a negative way. 'Would you like to play with this toy?', 'No'. Both kids know exactly where they stand.

But if an adult was in the same scenario, they might take that rejection of the toy as a sign that the other person doesn't like them and that they've never liked them.

Kids also aren't afraid to ask the question. They will ask whatever and as many questions as they need to in order to understand. They don't have baggage and *sh*tuff* in their model of the world that colours their communication.

When people become inferential they start looking to extract meaning from situations all the time. People do it without even thinking about it. It takes a conscious effort and a level of self-awareness to stop yourself if you have a natural tendency to do this. You also need to get to the root cause of what drives it within the filters that dictate your model of the world.

Now Your Turn: Interpretation or meaning?

Read the following sentences and write down how you'd respond if someone said them to you. Once you have written how you would respond, revisit
the sentences again and ask yourself, 'What is the literal question and have
I implied meaning that just isn't there?':

'I'm thirsty.'
'It's draughty with that window open.'
'It's getting dark, we could do with turning the light on.'
'Was that the doorbell?'
'I wish I had the money to go out tonight.'

You will find the full version of this exercise at www.be-more-kid.com.

CHAPTER 7

BEING REAL

When we talk about being real what we mean is being authentically you. It's about being who you are, being honest about what you're feeling in the moment and not holding onto those emotions. When we interviewed children for this book we just loved their authenticity and how they were totally honest about what they liked and didn't like, and how they just got on with things.

As adults, we're good at holding grudges, or generalising and expecting a particular outcome because that's what has happened before. This is all about feeling emotions, accepting them, and letting go.

Whatever that emotion is, you need to feel it. You've got to get angry, or upset, or elated and you've got to express it. It's okay to say, 'I'm angry about this'. The most important thing is to process that emotion and make sense of it so that you can let it go.

You can't just continue feeling angry, for example, and paper over the cracks because it's not healthy to hold onto that emotion.

The key is finding a way to genuinely let go. Most adults will say, 'forgive and forget', except they don't. Suppressing your emotions isn't just bad for your mental health, it impacts your physical health too and can lead to dis-ease within the body.

There's a growing body of scientific evidence[1] that shows how storing emotions can lower your immune system and lead to physical health problems in the long term.

This kind of disconnection also leads to physical tension in the body. As people get older, they tend to lose their ease of movement. They store up all those suppressed emotions and this manifests as tension within the body. They get tension headaches, their jaws are tight, their shoulders are hunched. All of this is a physical representation of what's going on in our minds.

Some people don't just suppress their feelings from other people, they won't even acknowledge them to themselves. We've heard it described as a kind of Pandora's box, where people are scared of opening themselves up to those emotions because it's been so long since they allowed themselves to feel anything that they don't know what will happen and are worried that they won't be able to cope.

One of our coaching clients said to us, 'I can't think about the emotions, because if I do I think that everything will just unravel in front of me'. That can be a very real and valid fear, but it isn't good for that person's physical or mental health.

WHAT DOES BEING REAL LOOK LIKE?

There are many public figures who we feel embody the kind of authentic, real, child-like attitude we can emulate. People like Alison Hammond, Simon Rimmer and Tim Lovejoy, Chris Evans and Richard Branson here in the UK, as well as the likes of Hugh Jackman and Keanu Reeves, all have a zest for life. They have a magnetic energy, they're playful, honest and open, and they're the kind of people we all gravitate towards.

Success comes to them because they're being real, they're being themselves and they're not afraid of saying what they're feeling.

---

[1] https://www.ncbi.nlm.nih.gov/pubmed/28703602; https://www.ncbi.nlm.nih.gov/pubmed/24871875; https://www.ncbi.nlm.nih.gov/pubmed/29488896

Ed's story

Alison Hammond is a mate of mine and one of the most natural, engaging and charismatic people you can think of. She's a presenter on ITV's *This Morning*, is a natural communicator and has an infectious zest for life. Her natural energy bursts out of the screen every time she's on. One of my favourite stories about her came from an interview she did with Hollywood star Dwaine 'The Rock' Johnson. They got on so well during the interview (mainly due to her warmth and energy), he ended up 'proposing' to her at the end of the interview. The next time they met (when he was promoting another movie) she arranged their 'wedding', conducted by Kevin Hart who she had arranged to be specially ordained for the ceremony! This was an amazing moment on TV but there are many more. Have a look on YouTube at her chats with huge stars like Michael Buble, Harrison Ford and Hugh Jackman. She gets so much out of her guests because of the way they feel when they are with her. It's not just famous people either, I've been out with her and you can feel the love people have for her, she naturally lifts people up and they feel so much better for being in her company. She's so warm and puts everyone at their ease – you can't help but gravitate towards her. Imagine the effect on all of our lives if we were all a little more like Alison!

We talk a lot in this book about people who embody 'Be More Kid', and you may be wondering what the tell-tale signs are that someone has 'Be More Kid' traits. One of the main ways that you know is that you can actually feel it when you are with them. It's so powerful, they have the ability to actually change the energy in the room just by being there!

Alan Barratt, CEO of Grenade, is a great example of this. He is larger than life, always positive, always smiling, open, authentic, engaging, warm and really puts you at ease. It's easy to see how these qualities, which he has always had, have helped him to grow the company that he co-founded

(continued)

in 2010 into the brand that is now valued at an unbelievable quarter of a **billion** pounds!

He thinks big, acts big, is very direct, enthusiastic and passionate. All of the qualities that we saw in the kids when we did our research.

Isn't it ironic when we are young that we are really eager to grow up, yet it is these child-like qualities that Alan has retained which have led to him attaining his amazing success! Alan's attitude is summed up perfectly by this quote on his LinkedIn profile: 'Not all goals have to be business related, I'm on a mission to reacquire all my favourite toys I had as a child ... Had to fly to Cornwall (any excuse) to collect this vintage Millennium Falcon.'

It turns out that it is possible to 'Be More Kid' and also run one of the fastest growing and most successful businesses in the UK. Alan is proof of what you can achieve by reconnecting with your inner child, he is an example to us all!

PLAYING A PART

Many people go through life pretending to be someone they're not. They put on a mask for the world to see and they try to live up to other people's expectations of them.

But that's really stressful. It causes dis-ease in your body because you're not being real. It's a very lonely place to be, because even when you're with other people you'll feel like they're not really with you because you're not able to be yourself.

THINGS WILL CHANGE

Once you start to be real and own who you are, things in your life will change. Some of your 'friends' will fall by the wayside. But that's a natural, organic thing to happen. You'll lose the people in your friendship group who bring you down or who expect you to do things for them.

What you'll be left with is the people who support you, and who you support. It's a growing process. You'll stop meeting up with people because you feel obliged to and you'll start letting those connections drop out of your life.

Kids can be very fickle in their friendships. They'll have a new best friend every week if that's what suits them best. They don't feel obliged to play with someone if they don't get on. They don't feel guilty that they're making new friends and leaving old ones behind, so why should you?

HOW TO RECONNECT WITH YOURSELF

If you feel as though you're disconnected from your real self, there are a few things you can do to start to reconnect. Start small. This isn't a process you can or should rush. Tapping into your emotions after suppressing them for years can be challenging.

The place to start is by just acknowledging what you're actually feeling in any given situation. You don't have to share your feelings with anyone, but just be aware of them. Be honest about whether you're angry, upset, happy, grumpy.

Look for those times in your life when you're suppressing who you really are. Do you feel like you're walking on eggshells around someone at work? Do you feel like you have to bite your tongue around your mother-in-law? Think about how you can express your feelings to them in an honest, open way.

It can feel like a brave step, but once you do it you'll realise that there's a lot of power in being honest. People will have more respect for you if you're true to who you are.

What often happens is that people bite their tongue, time and again. It's small thing after small thing after small thing until the straw that broke the camel's back. All of a sudden they explode about something seemingly trivial, but it's all those years of holding back coming out in one go.

This isn't healthy either. You need to start by acknowledging how you feel in the moment. See if you notice a pattern with anyone. Then you can think it through and do something about it. This helps you tackle it in a rational way. If you deal with it when you're emotional, you'll have a disproportionate reaction and say things you don't mean in the heat of the moment, and that isn't good for either of you.

NO FAILURES, ONLY FEEDBACK

You need to evaluate how you communicate. This ties in with the previous chapter about interpretation. But there's a phrase we hate: constructive criticism. This has negative connotations, shouldn't it be: constructive feedback?

But what you have to remember when someone gives you feedback is that it's only their opinion about you, or your actions, and that opinion is informed by their own internal filters.

This doesn't mean that you are what they think you are. They might think you're rude. Fine. It doesn't mean that you are. It's just their opinion and that shouldn't dictate how you act or operate.

Once you can appreciate that and say, 'Thank you for your opinion' and then move on, it frees you.

What you have to understand is that people will have opinions but those opinions will be based on what they're like and what's happening for them at the time. When you can appreciate that, you realise that their opinion doesn't impact you in any way. There's no reason why you shouldn't be authentically you. If you get in touch with who you are and gain confidence in yourself, you'll be empowered and will stop worrying about what other people think of you.

Now Your Turn: Your purpose

If you've lost touch with who you really are because you've spent a lifetime being someone else, it's time to reconnect.

Follow these steps and write everything down below each of the questions. Take your time with this exercise. It's good to go back once you have completed each step and make any changes that you need to, so that it feels, sounds and looks right and makes sense to you:

1. Write at the top of a page, `What is my true purpose in life?' Write down everything that comes to mind and note anything you feel a positive emotional attachment to.

2. Ask yourself 'What is it that I love doing so much that I would happily do it for free or for pleasure?' This can be anything; an example could be something as simple as ironing. However strange you may think the things seem just write them all down.

3. Now think about your hobbies and elements of your job that you enjoy, also consider the things that you see others do as hobbies and jobs that you would like to do. Write it all down.

4. Ask yourself this question, 'If I won the lottery or money was no object what is it that I would pay someone else to let me do for them?' With this question you are looking to find the things that really drive you rather than things done out of necessity. For example, someone may say I would cook meals for someone. Write down everything you think of.

5. Think about your favourite heroes, role models and others whom you admire; those who you would like to be like. Get inside their skin, what do they do or what qualities do they have that you want? Write down all of the qualities that you admire in these people.

(continued)

6. Now write down the things that others tell you that you are good at and also that you feel good about. Think back to things that people may have said to you as praise. For example, being a good listener or being positive or well organised.

7. Now, go through all of the things that you have written in answer to tasks 1) to 6). Look for any themes or recurring words and notice which things excite you most and which hold the greatest feelings of accomplishment. Look for the words or groups of words that stand out and make a new list of these. Now arrange the list in order of how much positive emotional attachment you have for each one from most to least.

8. Now, think about the things that you value in your life. Ask yourself this question, 'What is important to me in my life?' The responses you are looking for are words such as excitement, justice, fun, honesty, wisdom, etc. rather than listing things or possessions. The list that you come up with will be your values and principles that you live your life by. Once you have completed your list, go through each of them and put them in order of importance by numbering them from one to five, with one being the most important. Check that the top five really are your top five and if not, rearrange them.

Once you have completed Step 8, you will have a final list of interests/loves and passions that give you the greatest feelings of accomplishment that fit with your top five values and principles. You can now use this combined information to write out your purpose.

For example: 'I am a person who believes in peace and harmony. I get people together to bridge differences and gain agreement to move the community forward.' Or: 'I love animals. I feel happy when I help them grow and keep them safe.'

It can be any permutation and will be high level without any detail.

Now try it on. When you read it back to yourself, the words must look, sound and feel totally right and make sense. If not, amend them until they do. Your written purpose must really appeal to you and give you that sense of satisfaction, fulfilment and achievement.

Congratulations! You now have your purpose. Your goals in life should all satisfy your purpose in some way as this will assist you to lead a fulfilled life. You will find the full version of this exercise at www.be-more-kid.com.

BE MORE KID

When you look at how kids move, you don't see tension in their bodies. They're free, flexible and loose. They're not afraid of being themselves and they move with different friendship groups that fit with who they truly are.

We lose this ability as adults. One of the most telling questions we asked children and adults during our research was about holidays and why they took them. All the adults, almost without exception, said they 'needed' a holiday because they felt stressed and tense. They wanted an escape from their daily lives.

The kids said they 'wanted' a holiday because they liked going to the seaside, or playing with their family. They were excited about the idea for a whole host of positive reasons. They weren't thinking of it as an escape from anything.

We'd like to leave this chapter with a story about Glynn Purnell, the Michelin-starred chef. Long after he'd set up his own restaurant in Birmingham, his dad was clearing some things out and found Glynn's Record of Achievement from when he was at school. On the final page you had to write a personal statement when you were about 14 years old. This is what Glynn's personal statement said: "My goal is to have the most successful restaurant in Birmingham that all the rich and famous people come to, and people will travel from all over to try my food. I will cook for them every night of the week."

Now Glynn has that personal statement pinned up by his back door and he says it's what keeps him straight. No matter what he does, it reminds him of his first goal, which was to be a chef. He says that everything stems from that. Glynn is an author, a TV presenter, and regarded as a celebrity, but first and foremost he's a chef, which is the most important thing to him. And that's why he won't do anything that's not true to the goal he had as a child, because it's true to him. It's his authentic self.

CHAPTER 8

OKAY WITH NOT BEING OKAY

It's okay to not feel okay sometimes. But while it's fine to not be okay, this should only ever be a temporary state. Not being okay shouldn't become a way of life.

You can wallow in self-pity every now and again, but the crucial part is having strategies to deal with the negative emotions you're feeling. Otherwise you get stuck. It can feel like life will always be 'not okay', which can then become a permanent state.

Kids are okay with not being okay. But then they just get on with it. One minute you'll see them not being okay, the next they're doing something else and they're fine. They have this amazing ability to deal with some pretty big things remarkably quickly.

That's not to say they might not stay upset. Kids can still be upset but be getting on with their lives. They don't let these things keep them down. As adults we need to re-learn how to get over setbacks.

Adults have a tendency to go into victim mode. They seek support and they need to not be okay in order to get that support. Social media doesn't help with this. It gives people a really easy platform to reach out on; which can be a great thing for people to feel connected, but we've all seen the posts like, 'Could this day get any worse?' and then the stream of comments underneath, 'Hope you're ok hun', 'Just hang in there', 'Big hugs hun', etc.

WHEN DOES IT BECOME A WAY OF LIFE?

This ties back to what we talked about in the last chapter: being real. When you're honest about your emotions and you're honest with other people about how you're feeling, you can acknowledge you're not okay and then move on.

Not being okay becomes a way of life when people settle for things. Often it creeps in gradually. Remember we talked about the Grey Zone earlier in the book? For some people, being a victim is a way to break out of the Grey Zone. Seeking attention in this way breaks up the monotony of a humdrum life. This isn't a conscious thing that they're doing. Often it's outside of their awareness.

A good example of this would be checking into a hospital on Facebook but not sharing any explanation as to why. If things were really serious, you wouldn't check in on social media at all. So you have to ask yourself why you're doing that.

When you start to become consciously aware, you may see patterns in your behaviour or in other people's. Do you seek attention in this way? Are you feeding someone else's attention-seeking behaviour?

Bad things happen to all of us, all of the time. It's not just happening to one person. If you often ask yourself the question, 'Oh God, why does this always happen to me?' think about what's motivating that. Be aware that you're falling into a victim mentality.

WHY ARE PEOPLE NOT OKAY?

Forming an identity around not being okay can be a way of people feeling in control, or even being important, as it gives them something to speak to people about. When they are asked how they are feeling or how they are doing, they feel cared about and this gives them a sense of belonging.

Sometimes people avoid emotions completely. There are lots of reasons why they might do that.

Fear is just one of these reasons. As we have mentioned previously, it is often because they are worried that if they take the lid off the box of emotions, they may not be able to put it back on again.

They become dissociated from their emotions because they think they shouldn't show them. They've grown up believing that it's not okay to not be okay. But this applies to positive emotions too. They won't get excited or allow themselves to feel anything because they're scared of the negative emotions creeping in.

As we've already discussed, not dealing with your emotions often leads to dis-ease within the body, and sooner or later that will come out as a physical health problem.

Not showing your emotions is something that can be learned. If your parents dissociate from their emotions and don't share how they're feeling or show any emotion, you learn to be like this too.

The problem is, internalising everything that's going on and not sharing it puts a huge strain on you. It affects your physical and mental health. It's also very isolating and often results in feeling very alone, isolated and detached.

ACKNOWLEDGE HOW YOU'RE FEELING

There will be situations where it's not appropriate for you to express your emotions but that doesn't mean you can't acknowledge them. If you're in a meeting at work you can't just stand up and scream or shout, but you can leave the room later and reflect on why you felt like you wanted to scream and shout. Acknowledge your emotions, and process them to understand them rather than suppressing them.

That's the first step to breaking out of this cycle of not being okay – acknowledging the emotions you're feeling.

NEGATIVE EMOTIONS AREN'T BAD

Negative emotions are good for us because they show us where our boundaries are. Reacting to those emotions is good, as long as you do it in an appropriate way.

For example, let's say someone cuts you up while you're driving. You might shout, or wave your hands at them. That's fine. That's an appropriate response that allows you to express your emotions. What wouldn't be fine is racing after the person and running them off the road.

To handle situations like this, take a step back and deal with it from the point of view of being outside the emotion, almost like an external observer. That will result in being able to have a discussion rather than an argument where no-one gets their outcome. It allows you to release the emotion in a healthy way.

BE TRUE TO WHO YOU ARE

Part of the problem is that, as children, we're taught what's important but that might not be important to us as individuals. We see the Disney films that always have a happy ever after ending.

But that Disney idea of everything being happy and lovely gives you a false impression of how life should be. It means you don't feel like it's okay to not be okay, especially within relationships. What you have to recognise is that there are ups and downs, and life isn't like a Disney movie. No prince is going to race in and save you.

Thinking this way teaches you to put your reliance on other people for your happiness. It means people feel like they need to be with someone else because that's where their strength comes from. Whereas actually it needs to be about you and what you create for yourself.

FINDING THE RIGHT MINDSET

Accepting that it's okay to not be okay sometimes is a mindset. It's not one you stay in. It ties in with if you don't like it, don't do it. Live a life where you acknowledge your emotions; yet your emotions don't control you.

Being human, and being an adult, is about harnessing your emotions. Recognise that when you are feeling emotions, they are there for a purpose. Life will always happen. People will always cross your boundaries. What you have to do is be okay with that, don't ignore it, and work out what your emotions are telling you.

You need to be a cause for your emotions rather than letting them drive you. Always ask yourself what you can learn from that emotion. Do you need to change your values? Are your values serving you well? Are you doing things for attention? Are you being a victim? Does this stop you doing things that would bring value to your life?

For example, do you avoid driving on the motorway? Do you not go to the cinema on your own? Do you avoid joining a gym? Do you put off signing up to art classes? Ask yourself what stops you doing those things that you want to do and acknowledge any emotion that presents itself. Once you recognise what you are experiencing, you can work on it.

Now Your Turn: Why don't you do what you enjoy?

Ask yourself this question: What is it that you enjoy doing that you don't do?

Make a list of all the things that are important to you, that you make excuses for not doing. Now go back through your list and write next to each the reason you don't do it, including any emotions that you think get in the way, e.g. fear or guilt.

You will find the full version of this exercise at www.be-more-kid.com.

BE MORE KID

Kids deal with their emotions and move on. They accept how they're feeling, even when they're not okay.

We're not saying you should express emotions in the same way as a child, by screaming or shouting. But we are saying you should learn from kids about acknowledging emotions and approach them in a considered and proportionate way that is appropriate in the circumstances.

Take yourself outside of the emotion. Use the mindset of it's okay to not be okay, look at where you're at. Be honest about how you're feeling. Process your emotions and then move on.

PART III

UNCONDITIONAL LOVE

Unconditional love is widely spoken about, yet it tends to be referred to in the context of loving other people unselfishly. It's often cited as being about putting their needs before your own and helping others to feel happiness whilst expecting nothing in return.

Although in principle this can sound like a very commendable way to live your life, the reality is that it can be detrimental to your own health and wellbeing in the long term. This is especially true if you continually sacrifice yourself and what's important to you and constantly put others first.

When we talk about unconditional love in this part, we mean in the context of not caring what anyone else thinks or says and not having to live up to the perceived expectations of other people.

We think it's strange that while it's perfectly acceptable to give unconditional love to other people to enrich their lives, it's not a consideration for most people to give themselves any love, let alone unconditional love.

If you think about the dynamics within relationships, there are four main ways in which people will behave. One is, 'I will win so you can lose', the next is 'I will lose so you can win', the third is 'I will lose so you lose as well' and the final one, 'we both win'. It's that win–win outcome that we're talking about in the following chapters. This is what we should be striving for.

One of the ways to achieve this win–win scenario in your relationships is to unconditionally love yourself.

Some people frame this as a selfish way to live life, but look at it from the perspective that if you're not alright, you're not any use to anyone else.

Think about when you're on an aeroplane and you're listening to the safety briefing. When they get to the part about the oxygen masks, what do they always say? 'Please make sure you put on your own mask first before helping others.'

This idea of unconditional love follows the same principle. Your main responsibility is to you, because if you're not right, how can you make anyone else feel right? It all starts with you and this isn't a selfish thing.

Think about what kids do. They'll say that they love you and show that they love you freely, but they also demand that their needs are met and are taught concepts like compromising and sacrifice.

What happens if you don't put yourself first? One day you wake up and find that you're living a life of regret or resentment because you always put other people before yourself.

This has implications for your mental health too. If you spend all your time concentrating on things outside yourself and don't take care of yourself it can lead to mental health problems. Self-care is important.

In the following chapters we're going to be looking at some practical ways in which you can put yourself first. Giving yourself unconditional love will mean you can give unconditional love to others.

CHAPTER 9

CONTENTMENT VS. HAPPINESS

If you ask a parent what they want for their child, the most frequent response you'll hear is that they just want them to be happy. But what is this elusive happiness that we all seek?

We don't think that people should be continually seeking happiness. If you strive for happiness you will always fall short. Life can be hard, things can happen that are outside of your control and you will never be perpetually happy.

If you're hell-bent on being happy above all else, you'll try to find happiness even when the conditions in your life aren't right for it. How many times have you heard someone say, or maybe you have said, 'I will be happy when …' only to find that this particular thing didn't actually bring the elusive happiness? All that does is increase your anxiety and put pressure on you.

What we should be striving for is contentment and a sense of inner peace. It comes back to the idea of acceptance. You can accept what's happening in your life and you can still be content, even if things aren't going the way you want them to.

The difference is that happiness is often considered to be an end goal and many people only believe they'll achieve this when they have the next thing, whether that's material possessions, a nice house, marriage or a family.

They're putting all their hopes of happiness on external factors, whereas contentment is within you. You can have it any time you choose. You simply have to recognise that feeling content is within you, yet most people don't because they still think of life as a linear journey with an end destination of 'happiness'.

ARE YOU A HAPPINESS JUNKIE?

Happiness is an addiction. When people get what they call happiness, they're associating it with pleasure. This fires up the pleasure centres in the brain. These are the same pleasure centres that might be fired up if you took a drug like cocaine.

People get addicted to these happiness hits. Their brain is producing dopamine each time and they want their next fix. They attribute those fixes to things like buying the latest iPhone or getting a promotion at work. As soon as they've had their dose of happiness, they're looking to the next thing. And the next. And the next.

But the problem is, the dopamine hit doesn't stop the chatter in the mind or the negative self-talk. You have highs and lows. Periods of happiness are followed by periods of not happiness. The cycle is much like it is for a drug addict.

What we're saying is that you need to break that cycle and break your addiction to the flawed belief of chasing happiness.

HOW TO BREAK YOUR HAPPINESS ADDICTION

What you need to look for is inner contentment. This is a place where you're okay just being you. It comes back to a lot of what we discussed in the last part of the book. You need to be authentic, you need to be honest with yourself and those around you, and you need to be okay with not being okay sometimes.

Of course you'll still do things that bring you pleasure. But the difference is that you don't need those external fixes to fire off the pleasure centres in your brain.

Look at how young children behave. They are intrinsically content. They don't need an expensive toy – often it will be the small things that make them happy. The stick that they can pretend is a gun, playing outside, climbing a tree. They're not happy because of the external things they have, they are content because they're present and just enjoying the moment.

As part of our research, we asked children and adults to score their happiness from one to 10, with 10 being the happiest they could be. We also asked them for the reasons behind their scores.

More than half of the adults we asked gave themselves a score of six or lower. When we asked why, it all came down to external factors. It was all about things going on in their lives, or because of what they didn't have.

When we asked the kids, the responses were very different. The majority scored themselves at least 10 out of 10. One even scored their 'happiness' at that particular moment as infinity out of 10, what a great way to be!

When we asked them why, their reasons were all based around what was happening at that moment. One kid told us they were 100 out of 10 happy because they were wearing their favourite My Little Pony T-shirt. One boy gave a score of six because he wasn't looking forward to rock climbing, which was the activity they were about to do.

The difference was that the reason the kids felt happy – or not – was down to what was happening in the moment, whereas the adults based their scores on a range of wider factors.

The kids got their happiness and contentment from the moment they were in and their way of being at that moment.

What was very clear was that the adults were taking it out of the moment and looking at it from the perspective of the bigger picture and what they thought they should or shouldn't have.

Happiness is a state, not a goal, and you can access a state any time. So, you can choose to be happy or not at any time. Contentment and inner peace are ways of being and are generated from within.

DEVELOPING RESILIENCE

Developing resilience is essential to being content. You need to understand that you create everything around you and to be okay with that. You have to sort your *sh*tuff* out first and you need to be okay with not being okay sometimes.

When things aren't going the way you'd like, you have to be able to accept that it's not ideal and not what you'd choose, but make the decision that you're going to be okay with that.

Again, you have to look at how children cope in periods where things aren't going well. Even in bad situations, they're able to find moments of contentment.

Adults, on the other hand, are always looking for that end destination of happiness. That means that when something goes wrong, it has an impact far beyond what it should.

THERE IS NO 'HAPPY EVER AFTER'

When we're growing up we're often fed this idea of a utopia. The 'happy ever after' ending to stories. But in life this doesn't exist.

Fairy tales and movies feed us this idea of an ultimate destination that we should be trying to reach, but all that does is take us out of the natural state we have as kids where we enjoy the moment and rely on ourselves for contentment.

We are taught that there has to be something external, whether it's a prince/princess or winning the lottery, to give us that happiness.

Social media further feeds these ideas of the perfect life, of the end destination of 'happy ever after'. But no one will ever measure up. It's too easy to compare your life to what other people want to show you of their lives and think yours is worse.

In actual fact, contentment is within our reach because it's within us and we have the power to find it no matter what's happening in our lives. We just need to be okay with being us!

Mark & Nicky's story

We've spent quite a lot of time in India on holiday and what often strikes us is how people on the whole have very little in a materialistic sense. They often live simple lives, they have simple houses and they haven't got lots of money. But on the whole, they seem much more content than others who have more.

That's partly because they've learned from their culture to accept life the way it is. They don't have the expectation that something external is going to sweep in and make everything better. They don't have that quest of looking for happiness outside of themselves because they're just living life the way that they are and they choose to make the best of what happens.

THE HAPPINESS TRAP

Constantly striving for happiness from external sources forces you into a trap that's hard to escape from.

The more you have, the more you need to work to pay for things. You need to do more of the work you don't like to pay for the things that you don't own but that you need to keep paying for. It might be the bigger house, or the new car on finance.

You're on a treadmill that keeps getting faster. You have to work more and more. You spend less time taking care of yourself and you spend less time with the people you love and care about.

There's a lot of clutter in our lives. We accumulate things but we don't stop to ask whether we need those things or whether they make us happier. In many cases these things don't make us happier at all. They take our focus back to the external things in our lives instead of allowing us to concentrate on the internal.

Ed's story

When my relationship broke down and I'd been declared bankrupt, I left the family home with a plastic bag that contained a toothbrush, a pair of pants and very little else. You'd think a whole life being represented by a plastic Sainsbury's bag of belongings would make me feel quite depressed.

But I've never felt a sense of relief like I did that day.

When you lose everything, you realise how much of it doesn't matter. You don't need anything if you've got your health, your friends and if on the inside you're okay and you're content.

FINDING THE RIGHT PRIORITIES

We're not saying that you have to leave everything behind to reach this realisation. But we have all been there and experienced this realisation in our own ways, just like Ed.

Now Your Turn: Finding your priorities

We'd like to invite you to pause and think about what's really important to you. Make a note of everything that you think of.

Now review this list that you have written and ask yourself how you can have even more of these things. What changes can you make in your life so that you can work less and have more time to do those things? Are there things that you can get rid of for example, which would remove a financial burden so you can do more of the things that you love to do when you are not out working to pay for something that isn't important?

Sometimes you have to work backwards to engineer your life so that it's helping you achieve your goals. You will find the full version of this exercise at www.be-more-kid.com.

There's a wonderful story that sums up how we fill our lives with things that aren't important and over-complicate situations.

A city businessman goes on holiday to a beautiful coastal destination. One day while he's walking along a peaceful pier he comes across a man fishing. He's sitting on the end of the pier, with his single line, waiting for a bite.

He's already caught a few fish and is whiling away the hours expecting to catch a few more. The businessman approaches him. 'Hey', he says, 'You could do really well here with the number of fish you're catching. You could get some other people to work for you and you could even get a fleet of fishing boats. You could be very rich and have lots of money'.

'What would happen then?' the fisherman asks.

'Well, then you could build a canning factory and you could start canning and selling the fish', the businessman says, visibly excited. 'You could be very rich.'

'How would I achieve that?' asks the fisherman.

'Well, you would work hard and put in a lot of hours, but it would be worth it', the businessman enthuses.

'And what would happen then?' the fisherman asks once more.

'Then, you could retire, come out here to sit on this jetty every day and enjoy fishing', the businessman says.

The fisherman nods, gives him a wry smile and goes back to his fishing rod, just in time to feel a gentle tug on the line.

Whenever you start thinking about all these things that we think we want, you need to stop and ask yourself, 'What's the point in having them?'

Otherwise you could find that you're working harder and harder and committing yourself more and more financially only to try to achieve what you already have but don't appreciate.

Ed's story

There are times in our lives when we lose sight of what's important. My partner and I used to run a business together. It was all-consuming. Our lives were all about trying to grow the business, win new clients, increase turnover, hire more staff and so on.

There was one day when we both realised that our priorities had been totally misplaced. It was a horrible day and one that I'm not proud of.

We had a big meeting for a client pitch on the same day as our son's first big school play. He had an important part in it, and we were both meant to be going straight there after our meeting.

But the meeting overran. We were both looking at the clock and we weren't really present in the way we should have been. I kept looking at the time and thinking, 'We're not going to make it'. We rushed through the end of the meeting and raced out of the building. We had separate cars so we both drove independently to the school.

The traffic was terrible and we both pulled into the car park at the same time. The exact time that the play was over. I don't think there's a feeling quite as crushing as a parent as when you let your kids down.

It was that moment when we realised we were going about our lives all wrong. We didn't do a good job in the meeting and we let our son down. It was time to look at our priorities.

There were no winners in that situation. This comes back to whether you're a passenger or the driver in your life. A driver would never have scheduled that meeting. They would have done what they wanted to do, which was make sure they were at their son's play. They would have scheduled the pitch for another time, making a win–win situation.

HOW TO BREAK FREE FROM THE HAPPINESS TRAP

When you realise that you should be striving for contentment rather than happiness, you need to find a way to break out of this cycle of always looking for that 'happy ever after' utopia.

The difficulty many people have is that they feel unsettled about where they are in life, but they can't put their finger on the source of that unease. As a result, they get trapped in the cycle of looking for that external thing to make them happy.

But contentment comes from within you. To achieve this state, you have to look within yourself. The best way to do that is to focus on being authentic and true to who you are. It's about implementing what we talked about in Chapter 7.

You have to be honest with yourself about what you really want in life. And you have to be honest about what's stopping you from feeling that contentment.

As well as being honest with yourself, you also need to be honest with the other people in your life. Don't shy away from having a conversation with your partner about what you want from life.

HOW TO START THE CONVERSATION WITH YOURSELF

Before you can have a conversation with anyone else in your life, you need to be clear about what it is you want. You need to be able to articulate where your feelings of unease are coming from and what you need to change to find contentment.

We recommend doing this honest assessment of your life once a year. Remember the Wheel of Life exercise we gave you in Chapter 3? Use it here too. It's a great way of checking in on your priorities.

Now Your Turn: What do you want and what needs to change?

Start by having a conversation with yourself where you give honest answers to the following questions:

What is it in my life that I'm not comfortable with?
What am I feeling about this?
What's causing me this problem?

(continued)

Give yourself plenty of time and space and let things come to you. Once you've started answering these questions, go beyond your initial answers. Dig deeper into whatever it is that comes up for you.

For example, maybe you're in a job that you don't really want to do. If you ask yourself why you're still doing it, you might say that it's because you need the money. Then you have to ask why you need the money. The answer might be because you want your children and family to have a good standard of living. Then ask what's the reason behind that? Because you want to spend more time with them.

If spending more time with your family is what you want to achieve, is having a job you dislike and working long hours the way to get there?

This process is all about letting the answers come to you and digging into what's behind your thinking. You need to bring all of this into your conscious awareness so you can pinpoint what's working for you and what's not.

Without that specificity, you won't be able to change anything. You will find the full version of this exercise at www.be-more-kid.com.

BE MORE KID

Kids live in the moment. Look at what our research showed: kids were happy if they were doing something they liked or even just wearing something they liked. Their contentment and happiness comes in the moment. They don't overthink or chase it.

This also comes back to some of the areas we've already looked at. They don't do things they don't like. They're honest about their feelings. These are all things that, as adults, we need to re-learn.

CHAPTER 10

BEYOND POSITIVE THINKING

Positive thinking is just a start. On its own, positive thinking will do nothing. You need to take action. Seeing things in a positive way can be beneficial. What we're going to look at in this chapter is why we think positively or negatively, and how you can change that.

OPTIMIST OR PESSIMIST?

Is the glass half full, or half empty? It's a question we're all familiar with. If you see the glass as half full, you're considered to be a positive person, if you see it as half empty, you're considered to be a negative person. But do you ever stop to think about why people think differently about this?

Many people think you're born an optimist or a pessimist. They don't believe they have a choice. But this isn't true.

When you're a kid, you don't consciously frame everything in terms of positive or negative. As we get older, we develop filters and it's these filters that make us think of events as positive or negative.

In Chapter 6 we talked about how we develop our own model of the world. Our values, beliefs, memories, personality traits and previous experiences make up that internal filter and it's this filter that changes how we perceive what we experience.

This internal thinking is also associated with our internal feelings. These in turn are displayed to the rest of the world through our body language, external appearance and behaviour.

All the positive thinking in the world won't change your internal filter if you often revert to negative patterns of behaviour.

If you're going to change anything about your behaviour then you need to start by changing your internal filter. That means you have to explore your values, beliefs, memories, personality traits and the emotions you hold onto from previous experiences.

You need to change intrinsic things within you rather than just trying to reframe things in a positive light. And you also need to accept that sometimes it's okay to think negatively. Sometimes bad things do happen and you don't have to forcibly put a positive spin on your life.

The trouble with positive affirmations

Many people will use positive affirmations. They'll recite them out loud for five minutes at a time and they'll maybe do this three times a day. The problem is that many of these people have *sh*tuff* that they haven't dealt with and that they're not feeling positive about.

This means that not only do the positive affirmations not make them feel better, they actually make them feel worse.

The clue is in the name: affirmations. They are designed to affirm something you already believe. But if you don't truly believe your affirmations, all you're doing is repeating the things you want to change about yourself without actually doing what's necessary to make the change.

Dr Joanne V. Wood, a professor of psychology at the University of Waterloo, Canada, carried out research into dispositional self-esteem – one's overall feelings about oneself – and how self-esteem is perpetuated in daily life. What she found was that people who already had high self-esteem benefited from using positive affirmations. They already believed what they were telling themselves and this just reaffirmed what they already believed. The full article, called

Positive Self-Statements: Power for Some, Peril for Others[1] was published by the Association for Psychological Science.

However, among people who suffered from low self-esteem, positive affirmations actually made them feel worse. These positive affirmations instead reaffirmed all of their problems. It didn't matter what they said to themselves in the mirror because there was a negative voice inside shouting out, 'No, you're not'.

This is why affirmations don't work for a lot of people. It's because they aren't changing the underlying belief. That belief comes from the unconscious mind and it will always trump what you're telling yourself in your conscious mind.

CHALLENGING YOUR LIMITING BELIEFS

You need to get the buy-in of your unconscious mind to make changes permanent. To do this you need to examine where the limiting beliefs you hold come from.

Most people's beliefs and values aren't their own. They are imprinted by their parents or other very significant figures in their lives very early on.

And they never challenge them, they just accept those beliefs and as a result they're unable to change. Even if they consciously think they want to change an aspect of their behaviour, if that doesn't match up with their unconscious belief they'll never be able to do it and they won't consciously understand why.

For fast, effective change to take place there must be congruence and alignment between what we want consciously and what beliefs are held at the unconscious level.

A good example of this is quitting smoking. Even though a smoker might in their conscious mind want to give up, if there are positive reasons in the unconscious mind for them to continue smoking, they won't be able to quit.

They may have beliefs that smoking might de-stress them, or it might give them time out from the kids, or it might be a way of catching up with work colleagues. Without changing that positive belief and positive gain in the unconscious mind, you won't be able to give up using just your conscious mind.

---

[1] https://journals.sagepub.com/doi/10.1111/j.1467-9280.2009.02370.x

What often happens when people start to question their beliefs is that they discover there's no actual evidence to support them. That realisation is what's needed as a starting point to change the belief and consequently change their behaviour.

Now Your Turn: Identifying your beliefs

Here are two different ways that you can identify your beliefs.

Make a list of your beliefs. To make this easier, hold a particular context of your life in mind, maybe your career, for example. Write down what you believe in this specific context. An example from one of our clients is, 'If you don't work hard, you don't deserve success'.

Then ask yourself the following three questions and write down your answers to each for each of your beliefs:

1. What makes you think that?

2. What does that mean to you?

3. Does this belief help you or hinder you?

Alternatively:

Write down the beliefs/thoughts that you want to change under number one. Then, under number two, write what you want in place of the beliefs/thoughts you want to change. Finally, under number three, write a sensory-based description of what you will see, hear, feel and how you will behave when you have made the changes.

1. Beliefs/thoughts about yourself and your life that you want to abandon/change

2. Beliefs/changes that you will have in their place

3. How life will be better by making these changes

You will find the full version of this exercise at www.be-more-kid.com.

IMAGINARY CHAINS IN AN INVISIBLE PRISON

These beliefs that you hold, that have no evidence to support them, are imaginary chains that hold you in an invisible prison. They stop you from doing things. But when you break free of those chains you can do wonderful things.

We had one woman who came to see us because she had a fear of flying. We did the exercise of examining her beliefs and looked at what she believed about flying. What came out was that she didn't have a fear of flying but she had a fear of dying.

But the interesting thing was that when we unpacked her belief to that point she said, 'But I don't have a fear of dying'. That negative belief about flying just disappeared and now she flies all over the world and hasn't had any problems with it since.

Nicky's story

This is something many people have experienced. When my daughters were quite young and I was going back to work, it was the culture that a woman's place is in the home, that was restricting me.

I kept thinking that I should put them first, I shouldn't have a career and that I should stay at home with them. When I realised this was down to my beliefs and my thinking, I decided I didn't want these imaginary chains around me anymore.

I chose to start thinking about things differently. I could give the children a good life and still have a career. As soon as I changed my thinking, I got promotions and I was still able to give the children a really good life at home.

The idea that I needed to be a stay-at-home mum to do that was completely in my mind.

Evolve your thinking

What we'd like you to understand is that there's a difference between being a positive thinker and focusing on what you want. You can't solve anything with positive thinking alone.

As Einstein said, 'We cannot solve problems with the same level of thinking that we created them with'. This is the trouble with being a positive thinker. It means your thinking is only on that level and you're never going to solve the problems you face unless you can move your thinking onto another level.

We need to constantly evolve our thinking and constantly challenge and work on getting rid of negative emotions.

Imagine that you wake up one morning with positive thoughts about cake. You love cake and you start by thinking about all the different types of cake you could eat. You choose the best cake you could eat that day. Maybe you go on social media and find a picture of the cake you'd like to eat. You save it and you look at it, thinking positive thoughts about that cake. Do you have that cake? No.

You could ask all your friends what their favourite cake is and continue thinking positive thoughts about cake. But you still don't actually have cake to eat.

You might even buy all the ingredients for the cake you've been thinking about. But no matter how many positive thoughts you have about cake, you won't get cake unless you take those ingredients, put them together in the right order and bake them for the right amount of time.

Positive thinking is just the beginning. You have to take action. And not just any action, the right action to get the outcome you want.

How to go beyond positive thinking

You need to get yourself into the action habit. Making that commitment to do something is an important first step. Once you start the action habit, momentum builds and it's hard to stop. Once you achieve one goal in your life you want to achieve more. And that's intoxicating, especially if you're doing things that you previously thought you'd never do.

It all starts with action though. Commit to doing something so that you follow through. You don't have to start with big things either. Start small and as your momentum builds, the things you do will build with it.

Ed's story

I've done several things that at one point in my life I thought were out of my reach, just by making a commitment.

For example, I never thought I'd be the kind of person who would do a skydive. But a few years ago I did just that. I thought, 'I'm going to do a skydive'. And then I committed to it by booking it. As soon as I'd booked it my thought patterns around skydiving changed. I knew then I was going to do it, so I started to prepare for it.

BE MORE KID

As kids we don't have the same baggage clogging up our filters that we have as adults. Kids will naturally think positively, it's not a conscious choice. Adults, on the other hand, will try to force positive thinking because of all this *sh*tuff* clogging up their internal filters.

Kids haven't yet taken on all those beliefs that belong to other people. They can be anything they want to be – an astronaut, a ballerina, it doesn't matter. They really believe that's possible, and why not? Kids don't sit around just thinking about the life that they want, they take action and do things.

Adults tie themselves up in these imaginary chains and limit what they think they're capable of. All of the dreams they had as a kid slowly fade away and seem unattainable, that's if they even think about them at all.

We need to clear out our internal filters and go back to seeing the world as we did as kids – a place that's full of opportunity where anything is possible – and then take action to achieve the things that we want.

CHAPTER 11

THE POWER OF IMAGINATION

Our unconscious minds don't know the difference between what's called reality and what's called imagination.

There is no difference between what you imagine and what you think is real. Your unconscious mind is so powerful, it will believe anything you tell it.

That means that just by thinking differently and using our imaginations differently, we can change the way that we feel. This, in turn, will actually change what we see in our minds.

The lemon exercise

Please read the following text and then do as we suggest.

Imagine a lemon. A beautiful ripe, plump lemon, that rich yellow colour that really ripe lemons are. Imagine squeezing that lemon gently and it feels soft beneath your fingers.

You carefully take a sharp knife and cut the lemon in half. As you do that, the juice squirts and you can feel it running down your hand, you smell that sharp lemon smell as you lift the lemon to your nose and inhale that wonderful fresh aroma. Catching the juice that's running down your hand with the tip of your tongue, you taste that wonderful lemon taste.

Now close your eyes and imagine that. When you have experienced that exercise fully, open your eyes again.

How was that? Usually one of a couple of things happen with this exercise. Some people really taste that lemon taste in their mouth and others experience the sensation that you get when you taste a really sour lemon and it sucks your cheeks in.

That just demonstrates how powerful the imagination is. You will find the full version of this exercise at www.be-more-kid.com.

DO YOU KNOW WHAT IS REALITY?

In the last chapter we talked about limiting beliefs and how to examine where they come from. When you realise that many of your limiting beliefs have no evidence to support them, you can see how you've turned nothing into something.

Most of that happens in your imagination. You look for false evidence to support that limiting belief and it then becomes a self-fulfilling prophecy. You use this imagined evidence to build on your belief. As Henry Ford said, 'If you think you can or you think you can't, you are right.'

It's why we refer to the imaginary chains and invisible prison. They are just constructs of your imagination.

But the great thing about your imagination is that although it might be holding you back from living the life you want now, you can use it to help you change that and live the life that you truly want.

TRAINING YOUR MIND

There are many models of how our mind works. One of them is the notion that our experience is an endless sequence of memories that we attribute meaning to.

These memories are stored away, ready to pop up whenever they're needed. They evoke a physical reaction in the body too. So, with the lemon exercise it's why people felt like they could taste or smell the lemon. Their memory results in this physical reaction.

It's your unconscious mind that triggers this reaction in the body. That means if you can train your mind, your body will do what it needs to make that imagined picture a reality.

Look at the top sports people in the world. Before they have success, they imagine themselves doing it. Take the top golfers: they all have a habitual routine before they hit the ball.

The hitting of the ball is relegated to the unconscious because they've practiced it to the point that there should be no conscious thought about it. They just hit a golf ball. They know how to do that and they've practiced for it.

The routine before they hit the ball is where the imagination comes in, because a good golfer will stand behind the ball and imagine the shot. They will see themselves, the curve of the ball, the height, where it will land, where the target area is. All of that will be imagined.

They'll have this unconscious process where they move into taking their stance and they just hit the ball. There will be no further conscious thought about what to do because once they've imagined it, that's what's implanted in the mind to do.

YOU HAVE A CHOICE

For many people, that pattern of imagination is one that leads to negative thoughts. One of the responses we often hear is that people don't choose to do this, it's just what happens to them.

Our response to that is that although it might not be a conscious choice, the reason they always imagine negative outcomes is because that's how they've trained their minds.

That might have happened because of the environment they grew up in, or because of how their parents were. Whatever the reason, they've trained their minds to think about the worst cases, rather than training their minds to think about the best way things could turn out.

The problem is that your mind doesn't know the difference between what's real and what's imagined. All you're doing is putting your mind and body through all the stress of a situation as if it were real.

SEE IT THE WAY THAT YOU WANT IT

Kids don't worry about the future, they do things and see them happening just how they want them to. They are content in that particular moment, doing what they are doing.

What erodes this contentment, as we discussed at the start of Part III, is the negative cycle in your imagination.

Now Your Turn: Retrain your mind

Think of a specific event that you are currently concerned about.

Now imagine 20 minutes after the successful outcome of that event.

What will you be saying to yourself? What will you be feeling? What will you see? What will you hear going on around you? Make sure it is after the SUCCESSFUL outcome of that event ... and however you choose to imagine that turning out is fine, as long as it's successful. How much better does that feel? Notice that those feelings you used to have are now gone.

Every time you think about that event now, just bring up that picture of your successful outcome, with you hearing, feeling and saying those things to yourself that you have put into your image of your successful outcome.

Any time any other picture or thought comes into your mind, quickly replace it with this image that you have created and notice how much better that feels.

(continued)

Do this for all events that in the past you would have worried, been concerned or even anxious about; make sure they are specific events before you do this process with them.

Over a period of time, if you do this with everything you think of, you will retrain your brain to use that wonderful imagination that you have to see things turning out well, which will be so much better for your mind, your body and your general wellbeing, and will attract so many more opportunities, because you will be in an appropriate and great frame of mind to notice them. You will find the full version of this exercise at www.be-more-kid.com

What you also have to remember when carrying out this practice above is that it's irrelevant whether things turn out exactly the way you want them to, because even if something doesn't go quite as planned, your mind and body will be in a much better place to resolve any issues that do occur. This practice makes you more resilient to life and the uncertainty that it brings.

Mark and Nicky's story

About 10 years ago, Nicky and I used this technique before we ran our first-ever NLP training event. For us that was picturing the scene 20 minutes after the eight-day event was over.

The whole thing having worked out exactly as we wanted it. We imagined saying to each other, 'What a fantastic group of people. That went really well'. This gave us a great feeling inside.

Day one, we turned up at the hotel to get ready to deliver this training. As we were getting set up, I turned on the projector and the bulb went 'blink' and went out. I thought, 'Okay, fine'. I went to reception and told them what had happened. They said they'd call maintenance.

After a couple of hours, no one had come to fix the projector, so I went back to reception to ask what was going on. They said, 'Oh yeah, sorry, I spoke to maintenance and it's going to be three days before we can get a new bulb'.

At this point I could have had a meltdown and start worrying about everything else that could go wrong. But because I'd trained my mind, I knew it would be okay and we took it in our stride.

Nicky and I had friends who were telling us to complain and ask for some money back from the hotel because this problem could have ruined our training, but what good would it have done us to complain? What would our state of mind have been like? How would it have affected rapport with the hotel?

It would have wrecked our thinking for the whole training if we'd approached the situation like that, if we'd listened to what our friends were telling us. Instead, we just found a way that everyone could see the computer screen and the PowerPoint slides, and we got on with it.

Having this positive focus helped us to see other opportunities, rather than getting caught up in emotions and falling into a downward spiral that gets out of control.

COPING WITH A FEAR OF THE FUTURE

Anxiety is all about having a fear of the future. It's certainly good to deal with the negative emotions on the memories that contribute to it, but fundamentally anxiety comes from fear of what your mind imagines could happen.

People can even become anxious worrying about feeling that anxiety. The reason that happens is because they can see themselves getting anxious and seeing things not turning out the way they want.

Remember that we're talking about training the body to respond to the unconscious mind. Your body is a robot. If you've trained your mind so well to focus on what you don't want, as soon as you think, 'I'm going to be anxious', that's what happens.

It could even be that you're in an environment where someone says, 'I think you'll be anxious over this', or 'Don't get anxious over this'. The problem is that the unconscious mind doesn't process negatives directly. Just mentioning anxiety can be enough to trigger the body to respond to the mention of anxiety.

The body is a robot that's just responding by changing your physiology to match what we associate with the word anxiety. It will change everything on an unconscious level. Your breathing will probably get shallower. Your heart will beat faster.

All of those things will then happen because the body follows the mind.

BE MORE KID

Kids very much live for the moment. What we want you to do after reading this chapter is to think back to the way you lived as a kid, free from worry, and recreate that.

Children use their imaginations positively in play all the time. They really believe what their minds are telling them. Remember the power that has and look at how you can use it positively. Always remember that it will take the same effort whether you use your mind positively or negatively, but the results are totally different.

PART IV

PUTTING YOURSELF FIRST

When we're kids, our natural state is to put ourselves first. We're programmed to look after number one and to make sure we're okay. It's self-preservation.

It's only as we grow older that we're taught to share. This isn't a bad thing, but we're put in a position whereby we start to feel we can't put ourselves first at all.

This idea of sharing and putting others' needs before our own goes too far. We're taught that you need to sacrifice something in order to have a reward later.

The values society teaches us are ones of delayed gratification. Do your homework and you'll get good results. Get good results and you'll get a good job. Get a good job and you'll get a good pension. You always have to sacrifice and do things you don't want to do to get a reward later.

With this idea of delayed gratification, you're programmed with this notion that you should always put others first and then you'll get something back later. But this isn't how it always works.

In fact, this is often a trigger for a mid-life crisis. People give to their families their whole lives without ever putting themselves first and suddenly they hit a point where they start to think, 'Is this all there is to my life? Surely there must be more?'

At that point, they start putting themselves first, but often they do this to the detriment of others and themselves, and life can become a train wreck.

What we're going to talk about in this part is that it's okay to put yourself first. We're going to look at how you do that so it benefits you and the other people in your life. We'll explain that you need to put yourself first if you're going to help other people to get the best from their lives too.

Kids hold onto the ability to put themselves first for longer than some of the other traits we've talked about. As we get older, we all develop different reasons for wanting to please others. It becomes ingrained in our behaviour.

In everyday life you might not be running into flames from a burning vehicle, but not putting yourself first has all kinds of other negative implications. It can lead to mental health issues.

What we're going to ask you to do in this part is to take a step back from situations and ask, 'What do I want out of the situation? What's the win–win for me?'

We're going to help you strike the balance between doing what's right for yourself whilst still being able to help other people.

Mark's story

When I used to train newly recruited police officers in road traffic collision scene management, getting them to put themselves first was one of the hardest things.

I would write all kinds of training scenarios, and in these exercises they would always run into situations blindly, because they were putting others before themselves.

It was difficult to get them to understand that they needed to look after themselves first, because without them there wouldn't be any help. But what it comes down to is that if you run into danger and get hurt, then you're no good to anyone.

CHAPTER 12

HOW TO ADAPT TO ANY SITUATION

B eing able to adapt to any situation is an important part of putting yourself first. When you have this kind of flexibility, you'll be able to put yourself first while still doing things for other people.

This is about being mindful and thoughtful about what you want to get from situations rather than pushing everyone else out of the way and doing things in a selfish way.

We've said many times, life happens. Some of that is good, some of it is not so good. One of the main things we want you to get from this book is knowledge of how to start with a solid mindset so that the things that have bothered you in the past, or that bother other people, aren't a problem for you.

Kids don't approach life from the perspective that it's good or bad. In some cases that might be because they're encountering something for the first time, so they just don't know. But one thing that you'll notice is that kids handle each situation individually and treat it for what it actually is.

As adults we tend to define everything in life as being good or bad. But who's to say what a situation is?

As soon as you start to think, 'This is good', or 'This is bad', you set yourself up for a fall. Often situations aren't quite what they seem to be. The most successful thing you can do is interact with what happens and just treat it as an event. It's neither good nor bad, it just is.

Electricity is a good metaphor for what we're talking about. On its own, electricity is neither good nor bad. As soon as you plug a laptop charger into a socket, electricity is good because it allows you to use your laptop.

But if you accidentally put your finger in a socket and get electrocuted, electricity is bad because it's hurt or even killed you.

This example demonstrates how people attribute meaning to things that actually have no meaning. And that meaning stems from how they interact with the world around them.

When we talk about flexibility, we mean that you need to show flexibility of thinking and behaviour. The Law of Requisite Variety says that the person or system with the most flexibility controls the system.

WHAT TRAITS DO YOU NEED TO BE ADAPTABLE?

Kids adapt to new situations and things so easily. It seems almost effortless for them. The reason they can do this is because they have certain qualities and traits that we lose as we get older.

The traits you need to adopt from kids are:

- Excitement
- Curiosity
- Living in the moment
- Persistence
- Open-mindedness
- Don't 'try' to do things, just do them
- When something happens, it's soon forgotten
- Don't be afraid to ask questions
- They want to get on with other kids, they're not judgemental
- They have routine and structure.

Let's look at some of those in more detail. One of the most important is the last one in that list: having routine and structure. This is generally imposed by parents. It's things like bedtimes, mealtimes, making sure kids eat a well-balanced diet and drink enough.

Having a routine and structure like this means kids are at their best physically and mentally. They're getting enough sleep and exercise, they're drinking and eating sensibly throughout the day.

As adults, we often don't have that structure. And it's often because we don't put ourselves first. We don't tell ourselves, 'I need to sleep, I need to eat well'. Instead we say, 'I need to work more, I'll skip that meal, I'll have a late night'.

But that's a backwards way to approach things. You need to do the best for yourself otherwise you can't function at your best.

Being open-minded is also really important. When you're young and you're at school, you're learning all the time. But when learning comes down to us as adults, we often stop.

We make choices that result in us not learning. We watch trashy TV instead of listening to a podcast from an expert in a particular subject. We read fiction instead of books that actively teach us something new.

Tied into this is that kids aren't afraid of asking questions. Not only that, but they'll keep asking questions, sometimes even the same question, until they understand or get bored.

When it comes to getting along with other kids, they want to. They don't judge, they just invite themselves and get involved with the game. They're not afraid of how they'll look. That doesn't even enter their heads.

WHY DOES IT CHANGE?

Adults teach kids things all the time. We pass on our insecurities and fears to them through our actions. It's often not deliberate, but that doesn't mean it doesn't happen.

Because of social norms and their own programming, adults instil what they think is and isn't acceptable in kids from a young age. This stops kids being kids.

Think about this situation for a moment. How many times have you seen a child with their favourite toy who's told to share it with another child when they come over and try to play with it? But why should they share it? It's their prized toy. Adults don't just share their cars with anyone who shows an interest. It shouldn't be any different for children.

But this comes back to the behaviour pattern of putting other people first. By getting a child to give away their favourite toy to someone else, you've instilled the idea that other people come first in them from a very young age.

As adults who are role models to children, you have to think about what your actions might be teaching them.

FLEXIBILITY LEADS TO OPPORTUNITIES

When you're able to see events for what they are, and not label them as good or bad, you often find opportunities.

Ed's story

I recently met a friend for coffee and they told me that their car broke down on their way home a few days ago. For most people, that would have been a bad thing, a crisis even.

But my friend took it in their stride, called their breakdown provider and while they were waiting spotted a building nearby. So they went in to have a look. As it turned out, this could be a potential new training venue for them.

That's an excellent example of how being flexible in your behaviour, and not getting stuck in a negative mindset, can lead to opportunities. Life is just life. It's your interaction with it that will change you and make it good or bad. That's why you need flexibility of behaviour.

WHAT STOPS PEOPLE BEING ADAPTABLE?

NEGATIVE EMOTION

Negative emotion is what stops people from being adaptable. When people hold onto things, it builds up. Then there will be some trivial thing that is the straw that broke the camel's back.

This is why you see people overreacting to seemingly trivial things, because that is just the tipping point for a lot of things that have come before it.

It helps if you can understand how our minds work. Our mental filing system links similar events together. So if you stay angry after something happens and don't deal with that emotion, you carry it around with you.

You associate that memory with other angry memories too. Imagine that you have a cup. It's your anger cup. The more you pour into it, the closer to the brim the anger gets. If you keep pouring more in without letting any out, it's going to overflow.

When there is no more space in the cup you have no space to respond, so instead you react.

This is why it's so important to release the negative emotions associated with past events.

EMOTIONS IN, SKILLS OUT

This is when you see people react rather than respond. As soon as you get emotional, you forget everything you've been taught about the way you should behave and what you should do.

You will go into that emotion and that will have to play out until you end whatever it is.

The reason you feel all these emotions is because you haven't dealt with them in the past – you have stored them. So when that emotion comes out, all your skills go out of the window.

People become very behavioural and they don't have the ability to reason things through.

Think about your anger cup. If we go through life collecting these events and memories and storing all these emotions, sooner or later we'll reach a tipping point and the anger will spill out.

However, if you deal with your emotions as you go through life and keep the past where it belongs, you're able to respond instead of reacting.

Am I reacting or responding? That's a good question to ask yourself. If you're reacting, you're not in control. You're back to being the passenger instead of the driver.

Now Your Turn: How to get rid of negative emotion

To get rid of the negative emotions attached to a past event, that event needs to lose the meaning it had at the time. Here's an exercise you can do to help you let go of those negative emotions.

Think back to a specific event in the past that you're still bothered by. It's really important that this is a specific time when you felt really sad, or really fearful or really angry.

Think of that time. As you do, see it as a picture in your mind's eye, one that's outside of you. Now you're looking at that picture of that event and you're feeling those negative emotions.

Now push that picture away from you. Imagine it whizzing across the room and going all the way to where the wall meets the floor. Now imagine that picture shrinking to the size of a postage stamp.

Make everything in the picture dark and put yourself in that picture, so you can see the back of your head. Now imagine locking that picture in place.

Once you've done that, think about how that old memory feels different. What's changed?

We've changed the coding of the way that memory is stored, and therefore the emotion that was attached to the old picture is no longer present. You will find the full version of this exercise at www.be-more-kid.com.

PRESSURE

Another thing that stops us from adapting to situations is the pressure we put on ourselves.

People often have the attitude that they're always right, no matter what. It's always someone else's fault. This stops them learning from their own behaviour and that means they always repeat the same behaviour.

We can't adapt because we don't have control if we always think it's someone else's fault.

STRIVING FOR PERFECTION

Many people believe perfection is possible. That means we always have this sense of falling short of the mark, or that we've let ourselves down, or that we should have done better.

This can often stop people from trying something different, because they're scared that they're going to get it wrong, or let themselves down.

The idea of striving for perfection is something we're programmed for from a very young age. Exams at school condition us to always aim for one grade higher. A isn't enough, you need an A* or A+.

Our parents can reinforce that by asking why we didn't get an A+ when we came home with an A–. That's done with good intent, to encourage children to work harder next time. But it can make them believe that it's not even worth trying because they don't think they can meet those expectations.

Not only do we get set unrealistic goals, but the goal posts we're aiming for move. A couple of decades ago A was the highest grade. Now there is A*. What's going to come next?

GIVE YOURSELF A BREAK

You have to realise that whatever happened in the past, you did the best you could with the resources you had available at that time.

People often give themselves a hard time, wishing that they'd done things differently, but they only think that now because their thinking has changed and they've learned from the past.

If you went back to that situation and you only had the same resources that you had available at that time, then you would make the same decision again and behave the same way because you did your best with what you had. It's a learning process.

You also have to give other people a break. Remember that we're all different, with different programming. How you see a situation will be determined by your internal view of the world.

Even if you share similar values with someone, they will have different internal filters and will therefore see things differently. You can't expect someone else to behave in the same way you would because they aren't the same as you. You have to let go of that expectation of behaviour.

You can't judge other people for how they view the world either. People often say you shouldn't discuss politics, religion or children with your friends because you will just fall out.

But if you and your friends are all emotionally mature, why can't you discuss those topics without falling out? You should be able to accept that everyone is different and show that flexibility.

Now Your Turn: The keys to being able to adapt to any situation

Use these questions to help you examine your own programming and see what works for you.

- Can you remain in control of your emotions?
- When the situation involves someone else, can you stay out of the detail, because that's where disagreement happens? You need to find out what's behind that. Sometimes you might even both be saying the same thing but in a different way, and your higher purpose is the same.

- What's behind you taking a particular position? Is it driven by emotion? How can you get your outcome a different way? Remember that the more adaptable you are, the easier it will be to get your outcome in a win–win way for everyone.
- Do you take other people's comments or behaviour personally? Remember it's their *sh*tuff* not yours.
- Do you hold grudges or hold onto bad feelings? Remember that this harms no-one but you. There's a quote that's often attributed to Buddha, 'Holding onto anger is like drinking poison and expecting the other person to die'. Keeping anger in your body causes dis-ease and the only person who is negatively affected is you. You will find the full version of this exercise at www.be-more-kid.com

BE MORE KID

Kids are really adaptable. They find a way to slot into any new situation they find themselves in.

Kids also take situations at face value. They don't label them as good or bad, they just are.

Look back at the list of traits we gave you earlier in this chapter. Think about how you can foster those in your life to make yourself more adaptable. Also remember about the concept of putting yourself first. Give yourself the routine and structure you need to ensure you're at your best, physically and mentally.

CHAPTER 13

THE ART OF MANIPULATION

The art of manipulation is what kids do all the time, but they use it in a positive way for themselves. As they're growing up, they quickly work out who the soft touch in the family is and who they can wind around their little finger to get the outcome they want.

Adults often know when kids are doing this, but they don't like to say no because, of course, we all want the best for our kids. It can be really hard to say 'No' when they're pleading.

But the problem is that as an adult we can get into the habit of saying yes when really inside we're thinking, 'I really don't want to do that'.

We're not suggesting that you use the art of manipulation in the same way that children do. They approach it from the perspective of getting what they want, which often results in an 'I win, you lose' scenario.

What you can do as an adult is tap into that ability, but to create win–win scenarios within your life.

As well as looking at how you can use the art of manipulation in a positive way, this chapter is also about recognising when it's happening to you, learning when to say no and how to say no.

We need to stop saying yes to things when that stops us doing the things that are important to us.

DEFINING MANIPULATION

As a word, manipulation often has negative connotations. But you have to remember that you're attributing this meaning to it. Manipulation is often used in the context of doing bad things to other people.

But if you use it another way, it can also be what a doctor does to fix your broken bone. They manipulate it, and that's a good thing.

When you think about it, every conversation with someone else is actually a manipulation because we're trying to get our own opinion or thoughts across.

You need to consider the intent behind manipulation. In fact, rather than thinking of it as manipulation, it can help to think of it as influence. When you look at it that way, things change.

Being able to influence is seen as a way to get on in the world. Look at any of the leading people in the world, Oprah Winfrey, David Attenborough, they're all seen as being people of influence.

Having an influence that leads to win–win outcomes in situations is the key to being able to have a successful life. It's all about the intent behind your influence, not just for you but for everyone in that situation.

In this chapter we're specifically looking at how you can use the art of influence to put yourself first. That means you stop saying yes to everything and start saying no to the things that don't serve you.

WHY DO YOU ALWAYS SAY YES?

It's not easy for some people to say 'No'. It's how they get themselves into all kinds of awkward situations, such as taking on too much at work, or always babysitting the grandkids.

For some people it's the way they've been brought up, to always say 'Yes' and to always please others. To not put themselves first.

It comes back to the idea of societal conditioning, where you're put into a role of being a giver not a taker, or a nurturer, or however you want to frame it. It's a pattern of people-pleasing.

Never saying 'No' to anything can be really stressful. What we're asking you to do is look at what the real issue is. Why don't you like to say 'No'? Do you feel guilty? If you can identify what's behind your 'Yes', you can keep that in mind in the future. Remember the exercise in Chapter 5 – the power of 'No' – come back to this if you find you're constantly saying 'Yes'.

Mark's story

I'm one of seven kids. When we were growing up our mother always put us first and used that as an excuse as to why she led an unfulfilled life.

Even though she moaned about it all the time, she'd always look to please us and Dad. One thing she always told us was that she wanted to be a florist, but she couldn't because of us.

She lived her life with regret. And this is common among a lot of people with kids. They often do things they don't want to do out of a sense of duty. But then they get older and look back on all the things they didn't do, and they regret not doing them when they were younger.

This wasn't a happy place to grow up because we were always reminded of someone who wasn't fulfilled. It may have been out of my conscious awareness, but it was there.

I remember that Mum moaning about everything she sacrificed for us became something of a running joke in the family. I even remember one time when she was older saying to her, 'Right, Mum, if you want to be a florist you can be a florist now'. Her response was, 'Oh no, I'm too old now'.

But the other thing about my mum, and her constant sacrifices, was that she always expected something in return. She expected to have control and a say over things.

I remember when I was younger that if she didn't approve of a girlfriend, she would make their life hell. She meddled in areas of our lives that she didn't need to, because she felt she deserved a say.

> She put herself in this position where she always had the expectation that she should get something back. I used to call it, 'points in the bank'.
>
> I always felt like I was playing this game. And sometimes I'd do things I knew my mother liked just to get some points in the bank with her.

HOW TO TELL IF YOU SAY YES TOO MUCH

One of the signs that you've fallen into this pattern of always saying yes is that you're constantly seeking external validation.

Ask yourself whether you just know when you've done a good job on a task or whether you need some kind of external validation from someone else to know you've done a good job.

If you need this external validation it means you've reached a point where you may keep saying yes to things, because you want people to tell you that you're doing a good job.

SAY YES FOR THE RIGHT REASONS

Looking at this from the perspective of the art of influence, the best way to give, is to give without any expectation.

You need to give unconditionally, whether it's your time, money, possessions or anything else. Say yes to things, but say yes with a positive intent that you're doing it because you want to do it, not because you're driven to do it by your programming or something outside of your conscious awareness.

Make sure you're saying 'Yes' for the right reasons and that you give unconditionally.

If you think that you say 'Yes' too much due to factors outside your conscious awareness, do the following exercise to bring it into your conscious awareness. That will help you to change the things that aren't working for you.

Now Your Turn: How to start saying 'No'

Write a list of all the things you are currently doing that you don't want to do or that you feel obliged to do. Write EVERYTHING down, even the things that you feel guilty about not wanting to do. That might be childcare, or always being the person who cooks, cleans, pays for coffee when you're out with friends.

This list is just your starting point for change. Use it to bring things into your conscious awareness.

Understand that you can't change everything straight away. There can be a temptation to jump into action and do a complete about-turn on the things you've been doing to this point, much to the bemusement of everyone else in your life.

This can create conflict and arguments, because in other people's eyes and out of the blue, you're suddenly reeling off a list of all the things you're not prepared to do or don't want to do any more.

We believe in a transition, not a 'Big Bang'. You will find the full version of this exercise at www.be-more-kid.com.

LOOK FOR THE WIN–WIN WAY

The theory behind win–win comes from ecology. This is the study of consequences. It comes down to the idea that for every action there's an equal and opposite reaction.

We want you to create change in a win–win way. That means the changes you make shouldn't, as far as possible, affect the ecology of your relationships.

What you have to do when you take action is look at the consequences of that action. It could be for ourselves, for our nearest and dearest, for our family, for the city you live in, for your country, even for your planet.

For every action there are three potential ways of approaching it. There's the 'I will win so you can lose', which is often a way to exercise authority; there's the 'I will lose so you can win', which is abusive to self because you're not attending to your own needs and that's to your detriment; and there's the 'win–win'.

When you're looking for the win–win you have to ask, 'How do I win and how do you win?'

HOW NOT TO WIN

A good example that embodies the exact opposite of everything we've been talking about in this chapter, and which demonstrates how everyone loses if you don't seek a win–win, is the BSE outbreak in British beef farming back in the 1980s and 1990s.

The supermarkets started to play an 'I win, you lose' scenario with farmers. They squeezed the prices and put farmers under pressure. In an attempt to 'win', the farmers found ways to do things more cheaply.

That meant they changed the food they were giving to their cattle. However, this lower-quality food introduced BSE to cattle in the UK. This is also known as Mad Cow Disease and it's a condition that affects the nervous system of the cows.

Thousands of cattle contracted the disease and there were a number of cases of humans contracting vCJD, the human variant, after eating infected meat.

So the farmers tried to play the game of 'I win so you can lose' with consumers. But all that happened in the end was that everyone lost.

Consumers stopped buying beef. UK exports of beef were banned for years. Supermarkets had to import beef from overseas at a higher cost. Everyone lost.

Win-Win Requires Adaptability

Win–win is a true balance, but it requires adaptability.

Mark's story

I was talking to someone the other day about where we have our printing done. I use our local printer, which costs a bit more than some of the other options, but it's a trade-off I'm willing to make because they give a really good service.

In this situation, it's also a win for the local printer, because in me they have a customer who thinks they're worth paying a bit more for.

If everyone approached life in a win–win way, the world would go around a bit better.

How to Say No More Often

We gave you the exercise earlier of making your list of the things you don't want to do or that you feel obliged to do. We also explained that making changes too quickly can damage your relationships and upset your 'ecology'.

So, how do you get to a point where you can say 'No' more often?

Look for the Easiest Things to Change

Read your list carefully and look for the things that are easiest to change. It's important that you don't just transfer the problem to someone else.

For example, if you've been cleaning the house for 40 years and you suddenly tell your partner that you expect them to do half the housework, that's going to come as a shock.

This is about freeing up your time to give you more time to do the things you want to do, rather than transferring the problem to someone else. That can lead to all kinds of arguments.

GRADUALLY BREAK PATTERNS

If you've been doing something for a long time, then you need to have a transition period so that it doesn't come as a shock to other people in your life.

It's good to change things slowly and gradually set up new expectations. Look at how you can break the pattern gently.

For example, if you've always gone to a particular exercise class with a friend, there might be an expectation that you'll be there. You don't even discuss it anymore, you both just turn up.

In this situation you have to start to break the pattern ahead of time. So maybe tell your friend that you can't make the class in two weeks because you're doing something else. Maybe find someone else to go with your friend. Gradually go to the classes less frequently until you've broken that pattern.

The key here is letting other people know well ahead of time. That gives you a chance to broach it in the right way. If you leave it to the very last minute to tell them, you've got the surprise element and you'll get an emotional reaction.

If you've been thinking about telling them you don't want to go any more for months, and instead of giving them notice you just blurt it out one day, it won't come out right.

HOW TO DEAL WITH GUILT

If you feel guilty about not doing something, you have to explore what's driving that emotion.

Often guilt can be misplaced. We make ourselves feel guilty, but the person we're doing the favour for wouldn't want us to do it out of guilt. So just having that conversation and being honest can get rid of any guilt you feel because you realise there's nothing to feel guilty about.

Guilt is often rules-based, so it's important to examine what's behind that feeling. What are the rules? Often they're part of the programming we're brought up with, that you should act in a certain way.

As an adult, you need to revisit that and potentially reframe it. Those rules might have been good when you were a child, but do they still apply now you're grown up?

HOW CAN YOU MAKE YOUR LIFE MORE STREAMLINED?

The point of putting yourself first and saying yes to fewer things is to free up more of your time for the things you enjoy doing.

Look at other areas where you can free up more time. Could you do your shopping online? Could you hire a cleaner or a gardener? Could you find a job closer to home so you have a shorter commute? Could you reduce your working week by going part-time?

In many of these scenarios there are trade-offs, often financial, but if your life isn't the way you want it to be, you have to make changes so that you can make it work for you.

Nicky's story

This is an example from one of our clients to show the positive impact putting yourself first and using the art of influence can have on your life.

This client was always putting her family first. But this wasn't working out for any of them because she was doing it to the detriment of herself. She wasn't happy and that meant she was always shouting at the kids and wasn't getting on particularly well with her husband because she felt resentful.

She wasn't doing the things which were important to her.

After coming on one of our courses and doing some separate coaching with us, she realised that her partner didn't have this expectation that she should fully sacrifice herself for him and their family.

He was actually fully onboard and supportive of her. Once she realised this, she stopped feeling guilty. She got back on the promotion ladder at work and started living consciously.

We had a message from her recently telling us that she'd got a new job, that she's happy, her husband is happy and her kids are happy. Her health and fitness have improved too, because she's started going back to the gym. All because she's doing what's important to her.

There's a ripple effect. If you have successes or problems, it replicates across every other area of your life.

BE MORE KID

Making big changes, such as changes to your income, may require negotiations with partners, for example. Tap back into the skills that you used as a kid and use the art of influence in a positive way.

Look for the win—win situation and how you can achieve it.

CHAPTER 14

LOST DREAMS

What did you want to be when you grew up? What are you settling for now? What did you used to do when you were a kid that brought you joy?

Think about your answers to those three questions for a moment. The activities, films and music you used to enjoy as a kid can be a powerful way of reconnecting to and anchoring a state of happiness. One of the kids we interviewed wants to be the most famous YouTuber in the world – now there is a dream to excite you!

As we grow older, our lives get busier. People get caught up in the challenge of making it through each day. People have endless lists of tasks that they never seem to get to the bottom of.

The last thing we think about is doing the things that we really enjoy. They're always the things that get put to the bottom of the list, even though they're the things that we want to do for ourselves.

In this chapter we're going to explore how you can reconnect with your inner kid, reignite your lost dreams and find happiness by doing the things you used to love as a kid.

A WORLD OF POSSIBILITIES

Everyone's inner kid is different. What you reconnect with will be very personal to you.

It could be a hobby, playing a musical instrument, a sport, just anything you enjoyed doing as a kid. It's really powerful to go back as an adult and do those things again. It reconnects you with your inner child and reminds you who you are deep down.

There is always something really important to you behind those childhood dreams. Adults often lose touch with what they are though, and start to seek happiness outside themselves.

What we're talking about doing when you reconnect is firstly identifying those dreams and remembering why they were important to you. And secondly putting something new in place to help you achieve them as an adult.

WHAT STOPS US FROM FOLLOWING OUR DREAMS?

One of the reasons why people's dreams get lost is because of the beliefs they start to adopt from their environment.

A lot of that comes from society, whether that means your parents or your teachers at school. People want you to play small, they want you to play safe and they think they have your best interests at heart.

But actually, stopping kids doing something is the worst thing you can do. People start to say things like, 'Are you sure you want to do that?', or 'What if it doesn't work?', or 'I wouldn't do that if I were you'. As soon as you hear that regularly, all of your fire, spark and drive disappears.

All of a sudden, the older you get the less risks you're prepared to take; the less opportunities you go for; the less you dream; the less you do anything out of the ordinary. All because then you stand out and the people around you have probably told you that you shouldn't stand out.

When we're starting out in life we're very much about the things we want. As kids we focus on the things we want to achieve or the things we want to do.

As time goes by, life gets in the way and we stop thinking about the things we want to do. Instead, we switch to thinking about the things we need in order to survive and get by in life.

But often what people find they're actually doing is settling. The things they have in life aren't what they want anymore, they're not even the things that they need.

THE GRAVEYARD OF UNFULFILLED DREAMS AND INTENTIONS

This is where most people's dreams, and the things they actually wanted in life, disappear to.

It's where you'll find the book that was never written, the song that was never composed, the musical instrument that was never played and the business that you didn't start.

Often the reason why all of these dreams and intentions end up in the graveyard is because people are scared to take the first step.

People make excuses for not doing something. You hear them say, 'I can't do it now because ...' But using 'can't' is very disempowering. If you're saying you can't do something, that means you know the process of what you have to do. By saying you can't do this, that or the other, you're living with other people's effects rather than making the effect yourself. It's a sign of a limiting belief.

Another phrase you hear a lot is, 'I'll do this when ...' It might be 'when I've lost some weight' or 'when I've left my husband' or 'when I've got more time.' But it's just a fallacy because they may never have those things. Now is the time. There is an inspiring Chinese proverb – the best time to plant a tree was 20 years ago, the second best time is now.

People also say they'll 'try' to do something. But this presupposes failure, as we've already said, so you're committing your dreams to the graveyard before you've even started.

People need to examine their limiting beliefs and ask themselves, 'What actually stops me in reality?' If you don't do this, you'll end up with a life where you've settled, you'll feel unfulfilled and you're actually living in the graveyard surrounded by those lost dreams and intentions.

POSSIBILITY VS. NECESSITY

When you look at kids, they live a life of possibility. All their dreams live within the possibility of what could be.

If you ask a kid what they want to be when they grow up, they could say an astronaut, or a ballerina, or a footballer, like some of our kids said. They don't think about what equipment they've got, what training they've had, or where they live. They don't put constraints on their dreams in the same way that adults do.

Adults talk themselves out of things. They live a life of necessity, where they constantly focus on the must-dos. That's how their dreams end up in the graveyard.

They lose sight of their dreams because they get trapped in a cycle of trying to achieve all those must-dos. They must study hard to get a good job, to buy a nice house, to get married, to have a family, to send their kids to a good school, so that their children can study hard to get a good job … The cycle continues.

Another problem is that they tell themselves that all of those things are important. But the trouble with that is, everything else then becomes less important.

If you put importance on the must-dos, like buying a house, sending your children to a good school and so on, that means your dreams and wants become less important.

Adults are always waiting for things to become easier so that they can do the things they really want to do. But it never seems to be the right time. It's why people look forward to retirement. The problem is, by the time they get there often their most active years are behind them.

IN PURSUIT OF CERTAINTY

Adults are looking for certainty. They want certainty about what's going to happen in the future. But often to live your dreams you have to live in a world of uncertainty, just like kids do.

This need for certainty stifles your creativity and it stifles your wants and dreams.

Adults are also too serious. They live this serious life, as opposed to kids who have fun and get to do the things they want to do. Being too serious means you're dead to ideas in your mind and that also means you're dead to your dreams.

The trouble is that adults try to find certainty that doesn't exist. Life is uncertain by its very nature. We don't know what's going to happen next. Trying to control it is actually counterintuitive.

We're not saying that you should take off into the sunset and leave all your responsibilities behind. What we are saying is that connecting with your inner kid and the possibilities that your dreams bring with them, will lead to a more rewarding, fulfilling and content life whilst you continue to do grown-up things.

HOW TO CONNECT WITH YOUR INNER KID

The first thing you have to do is recognise what's stopped happening over the years. Many people fill every waking moment of their lives with something.

Chances are that their lives are so full of all the must-dos that they've forgotten what their dreams even were.

What they don't do is allow their minds to be free of the clutter. They're always filling pockets of time by watching TV, listening to the radio or staring at their phones.

Giving our minds this time actually allows us to connect with our inner kid.

One of the ways to get more free time is to implement some of the suggestions from the last chapter where we spoke about how to streamline your life.

Once you've freed up that time you have to think about what's important to you and use that time for it. Use the time to connect with your inner kid. Do the things that make your heart sing and the things that make you feel really alive.

Those things will be different for everyone. If you're not sure what those things are for you, think back to things that were important to you in the past. Maybe you wanted to be a ballerina when you were a kid. As an adult, that could be about finding a dance class.

Or if you wanted to be a dolphin trainer, that suggests a love of animals. You need to get back in touch with your dreams and find out what's behind them.

Now Your Turn: Reconnecting with your inner kid and remembering lost dreams

There's a caveat to this exercise: to remember your lost dreams, you need to have connected with your inner kid, otherwise all you'll end up with is another bucket list of things to be ticked off.

You shouldn't force this exercise. The more you force it, the more conscious it will be and that's the opposite of what we want to achieve. We suggest doing this exercise over a number of weeks, because it may take time to re-programme yourself to allow this to happen. It's all about starting to daydream again.

Begin by going out and buying a plain notebook. Then decorate the outside of it in any way that you wish. Use stickers, glitter, cover it in wrapping paper. It really doesn't matter. The important thing is that you're putting something of yourself into this notebook and making it just for you. It's the first step to connecting with your inner kid.

If you start to think that you don't have time to do this, so you'll just go out and buy a pretty notebook, you're missing the point. Or if you think this sounds too stupid or childish, you're also missing the point.

Decorating your notebook is about putting yourself into the right mindset.

(continued)

The next step is to plan time in your day just for you and your thoughts. This only needs to be 10 to 15 minutes in your day, although you can do it for longer if you enjoy it. You can go for a walk, find a quiet space on your lunch break or just sit at home with the TV off. The important thing is that there's no conversation and no background noise. It's just you, alone with your thoughts.

Some people find this whole concept very alien and wonder what to think about. So, below are some suggestions of things you can think about to get you started. Just allow the thoughts to come:

- Think about what activities you enjoyed doing as a kid. Think about what it was about doing them that you loved.
- Think about the dreams you had as a kid and have maybe lost along the way. What were they?
- If you could do anything and money wasn't a barrier, what would you do? What is it about this that you'd enjoy? It's often not about the activity itself, but what it represents for you.
- If you could take a whole day out just for yourself right now, what would you do with it? Anything that you feel you 'must-do' is banned.
- What hobby or activity did you always think that you'd like to do, but have never gotten around to? Or what did you used to do but have given up?
- What do you wish you could do more of? It could be something like baking, sketching, doing the crossword puzzle, reading or taking a walk outdoors.
- If you knew you only had a year left to live, what would you spend that year doing?

Write all of those things down in your book in any way that you choose. You don't even have to write, you could draw pictures, use symbols, even stick in photographs from magazines that represent your thoughts. It really doesn't matter how it's done because it's just for you.

The more you do this, the easier it will become and the more creative you'll get. Take your time with this process and enjoy it. It's not something that has to be raced through as a must-do.

Once you've connected with your inner kid and your lost dreams, start incorporating what you're finding out into your daily life. If you don't do this and take action, then they will just remain lost dreams. You will find the full version of this exercise at www.be-more-kid.com.

BE MORE KID

Kids embrace uncertainty and live a life full of possibilities. They don't put constraints in the way of doing what they want to and they certainly don't have a list of 'must-dos'.

Connecting with your inner kid can help you recapture that spark and ignite passions you'd forgotten about.

Remember that however your life has been up to now, and however far away you are from your inner kid, there is hope for a different future. That's what we'll be sharing with you in the next part of the book.

Hold fast to dreams for if dreams die, life is a broken-winged bird that cannot fly.

—Langston Hughes

PART V

LIGHT AT THE END OF THE TUNNEL (AND IT'S NOT ANOTHER TRAIN)

There is hope. That's what this part of the book is all about. Whenever you're experiencing bad times and you're getting close to the end of that period, there's the saying 'There is light at the end of the tunnel'. You feel as though you're getting close to solving the problem because you can see that light.

But just because there's light, that doesn't mean it's the end. The light could be another train coming the other way. So this is about accepting that although there will be light at the end of the tunnel, there may be other things you need to deal with on your way to it; there may be a number of false dawns.

But it's also about accepting that maybe you don't need to reach that light at the end of the tunnel. Maybe there are stops en route that will give you far more than you realise.

Often people can feel stuck in life. They wait to find out what their destination is before they set off. But life is a journey, not a destination. You need to set off in order to keep moving forward and once you're moving forward there is hope.

Once you're on your journey, you'll start to gather resources that can help you. This is as much about developing your resilience to those 'false dawns' as it is about reaching the end of the tunnel.

It's also worth remembering that you can't see the destination until you're on the way. It only appears when you're so far down the route.

You might even have a few options about where to go. This isn't about looking for the right way. There are just options and you choose one.

People often say, 'I need to decide what I'm going to do with my life'. It's as if they're just waiting to establish the end destination, the final outcome.

But there's nothing wrong with changing your mind after you've set off. You can enjoy the tunnels, wrong turns and cul-de-sacs.

Have fun exploring the so-called 'wrong way', because it's not right or wrong, it's just another way that you've explored and it's all part of the journey. You will learn things you can carry forward into the next stage of your journey.

Everyone can look back on their life and think of something that, at the time, felt like a failure or was a painful experience or something that just didn't work.

But how many times have you also thought, 'That was horrendous, but if I hadn't done that, I wouldn't have learned this. And that really came in handy when I went on to do this'.

When you look back with hindsight, even painful experiences can take on a positive light, because you realise that without them you wouldn't be where you are now.

Kids don't have this same attachment to an end destination. Watch the way they behave and you'll see that they're just enjoying the journey. Sometimes that might take them somewhere they don't want to go, but they never lose hope that things will get better. What they do is keep moving forward. They're not waiting to see the light at the end of the tunnel before they venture into it – they're excited to explore the tunnel itself and see where it leads.

You *can* teach an old dog new tricks.

Everyone is familiar with the phrase, 'You can't teach an old dog new tricks', but that's not true. It's never too late to make changes in your life, the only barrier to that change is you.

We aren't the change police and if people don't want to make changes to their lives then that's fine. But what we'd like you to do is admit that change is possible if you want it.

As soon as you admit to yourself that it's possible to change, you'll feel empowered. You have to realise that it's a choice to stay as you are. If you think that you're stuck and have no choice, you're not the driver in your life.

This part is for those of you who want to make changes, whatever state you think your life is in right now. You have the power in your life and the outcome you're looking for is probably closer than you think. This is about gathering the resources you already have, developing your resilience and finding a way to move forward in any direction. There is light at the end of the tunnel, and it's not another train.

CHAPTER 15

MUM KNOWS BEST

When you were growing up, we're sure that your mum (and dad) used to come out with phrases that you disregarded as a kid. We all know the ones, the phrases that just roll off the tongues of our parents. But the thing is, many of the things your mum told you do actually work.

We thought it would be interesting to remind you of some of those phrases – and we're sure you'll have plenty to add from your own collection.

It's interesting to look back at these phrases with adult eyes because when we're young we tend to dismiss them. But when you look at them now, you'll see how they can assist you to move forwards.

This part of the book is all about hope and light at the end of the tunnel. This chapter comes courtesy of voices from the past.

It's not about looking at the past and blaming yourself for not listening when you were young, or about blaming others for where your life is now. It's about using the resources you were given in the past to help you build a better future.

'NO SUCH WORD AS CAN'T'

Although this phrase can be irritating to hear as a child, it's hugely beneficial to understand how empowering this statement is.

What you come to understand as an adult is that in order to be processing what you can't do, you must actually know inside you what to do, otherwise it would be outside of your awareness.

The more appropriate mindset would be that you're choosing not to do something, rather than saying you can't do it.

By saying you can't do something, you're putting yourself in a stuck state where you remain the passenger. As soon as you realise that there's always a choice, you take back control and become the driver.

There's always a way. When your unconscious mind hears the word 'can't' it puts up a block and that's what stops you achieving something.

Think about the context in which your parents used that phrase when you were a child. Chances are they were saying it to encourage you to just get on with things and not be limited by your own thinking and beliefs.

'YOUR SCHOOL DAYS ARE THE BEST YEARS OF YOUR LIFE'

We don't agree that the time you spent at school is necessarily the best time of your life. For many people, school wasn't always enjoyable.

But when we dig into this phrase it's more about the kind of mindset you had when you were at school than what actually happened during your school days.

Particularly in your early years at school, you're full of awe at the world around you and you're experiencing everything with a child-like excitement and the joy of possibility.

When you're at school, you don't have the weight of the world on your shoulders. You're much closer to all the resources you have naturally and, as a result, you're more efficient because you don't overcomplicate things and wear yourself down.

Three to five is the age when you're still your authentic self, before the influences in your environment, society and the important people in your life start to creep in. But even when you're a little older and still at school, you're still a lot closer to that authentic self than you are by the time you hit your mid-20s or 30s.

Nicky's story

Children are being programmed out of creativity at younger and younger ages.

I can even see it happening to my granddaughter. I took her out for lunch for her fifth birthday and at the restaurant she was given one of those colouring sheets and some crayons.

The last time I took her out, she coloured things in whatever colour she wanted. But this time she was saying things like, 'Nanny, what colour do I need to do this? I need to colour the lettuce green don't I?' I said, 'Jessica, you can make those any colour you want'. Her reply was, 'Yes, but that's not its proper colour, is it?'

Already at the age of five that programming about what's acceptable and what's not is there.

It's the three-to-five-year-old mentality we're trying to tap into. The time in your life when you were authentically you without any constraints.

'IF IFS AND ANDS WERE POTS AND PANS, WE'D BE WASHING UP FOREVER'

This refers to not just wishing for things, but actually doing something to achieve them. You can have the best intentions in the world, but intentions don't get you results.

You'll get nowhere because 'ifs and ands' don't involve action. You'll be stuck in a cycle of inaction, sitting on the settee believing that the universe will bring everything to you.

'DON'T WISH YOUR LIFE AWAY'

Remember how it felt when you were young and you were waiting for your birthday to arrive. Or how excited you were on Christmas Eve waiting for Father Christmas to come. Or how you feel the day before you go on holiday.

It just feels like that day will never arrive and it's really hard to just stand still. We've all probably wished time away, and then we're told, 'You'll end up wishing your life away'.

When you're an adult, you see it differently because time seems to speed up the older we get.

The other trouble with always wishing for something in the future is that you stop enjoying the present. As we've talked about already, if you don't have the tools and techniques to master your mindset, that's where stress and anxiety start to creep in, because you're either living in the past or the future.

If you live authentically enjoying the present, you're at ease with yourself and there is no stress.

But there's another interpretation that we don't appreciate when we're a kid, in that all of those wishes you make when you blow out the birthday candles or see a shooting star, are nothing more than wishes and dreams unless you take action to make them happen.

It's about getting into the right mindset of taking appropriate action to make your wishes and dreams happen.

'IT'S NOT WHAT HAPPENED, BUT WHAT HAPPENS NEXT THAT MATTERS'

This is one that Mark's mum used a lot and is a great phrase to revisit as an adult, especially when you're giving yourself a hard time for doing something you wish you hadn't done or making a mistake.

When you take the learning from what happened and use it as a resource in the future, you view experiences like that very differently.

It's also about escaping from this idea of perfection. You're not perfect, we're not perfect, nobody's perfect.

Stopping this focus on the past will stop you apportioning blame. If you stop worrying about what has happened, it puts you back in control. You can't control what's in the past, but you are in total control of what you now choose to do as a result of that.

So give yourself a break, take those learnings and use them to create what you want in the future.

'IF YOU CAN'T SAY SOMETHING NICE, DON'T SAY ANYTHING AT ALL'

This one is about everyone trying to do the best they can with the resources they have. If you see the world in that way, it helps you deal with situations.

If you're in a situation you don't like, or someone says something to you that you don't like, don't take it as a personal attack. Take a moment to consider what you're going to say next. Ask yourself, 'Is it nice? Is it helpful? Is it a good thing to say? Is it going to make the situation better? Is it going to make them feel better? Is it going to make me feel better? Is it win–win?' If the answer to any of those questions is 'No', then don't say it.

All that happens if you do say those things is that you put more anger out into the world and you also internalise it. It makes you angry, stressed and upset. That has a negative effect on you.

If you can accept that the other person is just doing their best, and that it says more about them than it does about you, then you can go about your life as most kids do, not dwelling on things or taking anything too personally.

This is also about not treating other people's opinions as more valuable than your own. They're only coming at things from their model of the world. They don't know your model of the world any more than you know theirs.

Another phrase that often crops up, and that links in with this, is 'Treat other people how you want to be treated'.

Following that approach means you're projecting your model of the world onto everyone else. What you should actually be doing is treating other people how they want to be treated.

To do that, you have to assume that everyone is doing their best and you have to understand that people will come from different perspectives to your own.

Ed's story

My son Jack is 16 and I've had to have this conversation with him, about thinking about situations from other people's perspectives.

I received an email from a teacher at Jack's school about how he and a few other boys were really badly behaved in a revision class. She said they weren't really paying attention, they were eating and that it's not the behaviour she expects.

At the end of the email she explained that she doesn't get paid for teaching those revision classes. She gave up two days of her holiday to teach the classes, as well as another day to prepare. She ended the email saying, 'I gave up three days of my holidays and I didn't get paid for it, and that's how he chose to act'.

I spoke to Jack about it and his immediate response was that the teacher was overreacting. He said he and his friends were just talking a little bit towards the end of the day when they were tired.

But then I explained what was in her email, about how she'd given up her time to help them and how all that she wanted was for them to concentrate in that time she was sacrificing.

When he understood her side of the situation, her view of the world, he got it. He knew she wasn't just being mean, but could understand why she got frustrated with their behaviour.

'WE'LL CROSS THAT BRIDGE WHEN WE COME TO IT'

This is a great phrase. It's a reminder that people often worry about things turning out badly, when that situation hasn't happened yet. It comes back to what we talked about near the start of the book, about overthinking.

Instead of worrying about the potential bad outcomes, focus instead on everything turning out just the way you want it to. Do everything within your control and that you can influence to make it happen that way.

Once you've done that, just forget about it, because there's nothing more you can do.

It's also about understanding that, although there might be external circumstances you can't control, you have the resources you need to deal with anything that comes up and you can cross that bridge when you come to it.

'WHERE THERE'S A WILL, THERE'S A WAY'

If something is important enough, you will find a way to make it happen. If it's not important then rather than finding excuses, just be honest and tell people that it's not for you.

Rather than saying you can't do something, ask yourself the question, 'How can I make this happen?' Then you actually have to do what it takes.

If there are things that you need to do that you need external assistance with, always ask the question. Don't assume that people will say, 'No'. You'll be surprised by how much support you get when you actually ask people the question. Other people can't help you if you don't ask.

Mark, Nicky and Ed's story

That phrase – where there's a will, there's a way – explains why you're reading this book today. We first talked about writing a book together several years ago.

We all thought it was a great idea but then we all had a lot of stuff going on. We kept saying we'd try to meet up, or we'd try to talk and of course we didn't. A year or so went by without anything happening at all.

It took all of us saying, 'This is a great idea, we need to make it happen', for us to sit down and work on the book. It's important to understand that all three of us probably had more going on while we were writing this book than we ever have, but we've found a way to set aside the time to do it and to make it work for us.

We made it a priority and as soon as we did that, we found time to fit it into our lives. Where there's a will, there's a way.

You have to make things important. You have to get rid of the superfluous goals that other people think you should have and focus on the ones that have a positive emotional charge, that get you excited.

When you do that, you'll find a way to make them happen. This is also about recognising when you need outside help, whether that's from a coach, a mentor, or someone who's been where you are before. They are part of that 'way' to make things happen.

'THERE'S ONLY ONE PERSON YOU CAN TRUST IN THIS LIFE AND THAT'S YOURSELF'

Another phrase that's along similar lines is, 'If you want something doing, then do it yourself'.

Both relate to this idea that no one should have your interests at heart more than you. Your life is your responsibility and you can't blame someone else if you don't have your life the way you want it.

But there's a distinction to be made between taking responsibility for yourself, so that you're the driver, and not asking for help when you need it. So if you're in business and you have more work than you can deal with, or there's a skillset that you're missing, you need to bring people onboard to help with that.

It's also about accepting that you can only control you and your bit. In some situations, such as when you're a parent, you have to let the other person do their part too.

It's important to accept that you can't control them, but if there's something you're not happy about then your choice is to have a conversation about that and be honest. You might not change things, but at least you have controlled your part.

This isn't about pointing the finger and blaming someone else. It's about understanding that you're the only person who truly understands you and knows how you interact with the world.

It's about taking responsibility and knowing that if you made a choice, it was the best one available with the resources you had at the time.

If you believe that no one else can do something as well as you, understand that unless you help them improve, they're never going to get better. They'll only ever be able to do the best they can with the resources they have.

So this is also about sharing how you'd do something to help them and to make sure you're not limiting their resources. The results that you get back from anyone are dependent on what you communicate to them.

'YOU CAN'T JUDGE A BOOK BY ITS COVER'

The challenge with this is that if you don't like the cover of a book, you're unlikely to get as far as reading it.

When you relate this to people, have you ever thought that you didn't like someone, only to find out that they're really nice and you actually have lots in common?

We're drawn to the familiar, but if you step outside of what is comfortable for you then you'll expand your model of the world and your experiences. You never know what's out there if you don't do something different.

This is actually one of the things that kids do and it's a habit we have to unlearn as we become adults. Children will often make a snap judgement about whether they like something or not. Look at how they respond to food. It's not uncommon to hear a kid saying they don't like something they've never tried, just because they think all green things are yucky, for instance.

As an adult we need to think differently and re-programme ourselves. Otherwise we'll keep making those snap judgements and will go through life proving ourselves right.

It's also about not letting those judgements stop us from doing things. You may not let yourself experience new things if they're similar to something you've tried in the past and not enjoyed, for instance.

Kids are much more likely to just get on and do things, unless they're given that limitation by someone else. As adults we can learn from that, so we don't deprive ourselves of experiences.

BE MORE KID

Now that we've explored some of the phrases we were programmed to accept as kids, you can see we've got some great resources.

These resources can help us move forward and they're all tucked away in our childhood memories. By bringing them into your consciousness, you can see whether you've been using them, and whether there are any that can be useful.

Once you're connected to them you can understand where your thinking is coming from. You can get the most from those pieces of wisdom from your own parents and you can get rid of any that don't serve you.

This chapter might also make you realise that you have more resources than you thought, and as a result may be closer to the light at the end of the tunnel. When you begin to recognise that you have what you need for the journey, the next step becomes easier.

CHAPTER 16

JUST FOR FUN

This chapter is all about having fun, for no other reason than it's fun. It's about enjoying life, just for fun. It's about doing something just for fun because you want to.

There are some people who've retained their youthful approach to life, regardless of their age. We've talked about them in previous chapters. They're the people who are great to be around, who are frequently the envy of family, friends and colleagues because they always seem to be going somewhere or doing something interesting.

When looking at these people from the outside in, they're often told that they're lucky, or that they have an easy life, suggesting they've had privileges and opportunities made exclusively available to them.

Because we're so fascinated by human behaviour, we've researched the qualities that these happy-go-lucky people have in common. We're sure you won't be surprised to learn that they share the traits we've identified in our research with kids.

What it comes down to is that these happy-go-lucky people have retained certain traits from their childhood. The qualities they have in common are:

- Curiosity
- Sense of adventure

- Excitement
- Passion

How hard is it to talk a kid out of something when they've made up their mind that they want it? As we've said earlier in this book, for kids, doing something they enjoy will always take priority over something they must do.

Give them a choice between doing their reading homework or going outside and splashing in puddles and we all know which one would win.

Take a moment to think of some people you know who fit this mould. Famous names like Olly Murs, Lionel Ritchie, David Walliams and Ellen Degeneres come to mind for us.

It's important to understand that these happy-go-lucky people aren't like that because they've got lots of money or anything materialistic, they're like that because of a choice they've made.

Start thinking about what it is about those people in your life that you buy into, and how you can bring it out in yourself.

Because the thing is, if you adopt what we're talking about in this book, you'll not only make yourself feel better, but you'll make other people feel better and happier too.

ATTITUDE AND RESILIENCE

One of the big differences between happy-go-lucky people and almost everyone else is their attitude. No matter what life throws at them they still seem to come out smiling.

It's not that what life throws at them is any different to what it throws at other people, it's their attitude that sets them apart. They treat events as isolated incidents, not another entry on a long list of 'bad things' that have happened to them.

They use the resilience they've built up, to get them through the tough times. They don't focus on the bad. In fact, they're unlikely to even mention the things that have gone wrong.

Conversely, we all know those people who will reel off a list of the bad things in their lives and will tell anyone who'll listen how terrible things are for them. It can be exhausting to be on the receiving end of that.

Now Your Turn: How do you answer the question, 'How are you?'

We all know people who will answer the question, 'How are you?' with, 'I'm fantastic, how are you?'

We all also know people who will answer the question, 'How are you?' with, 'Not bad', 'I'm surviving', or 'I'm still alive', or 'It'll be okay on Friday'.

When you hear someone respond negatively like that, it impacts on your own positive focus.

This exercise is very simple. Whenever someone asks, 'How are you?', think of a way of answering with 'I'm fantastic', or 'I'm amazing, everything's great, how are you?'

Find a positive response to the question and pay attention to the response you get. Similarly, when you ask someone else how they are, notice how their response makes you feel. Remember you only want to have a positive impact on yourself and others. You will find the full version of this exercise at www.be-more-kid.com.

HOW TO DEVELOP RESILIENCE

There are several ways in which happy-go-lucky people get their resilience. They're all things you can do to develop your resilience too.

From the research we've done, they get their resilience in a number of ways:

- They make time for the things they enjoy.
- They spend time with people who add value to their lives.
- They make even the most boring and mundane tasks fun.
- They get good-quality and sufficient sleep.
- They look after their health.
- They learn tools and techniques that allow them to master their mindset.

All of those things will impact on how they feel within themselves. They take care of themselves. This means that when things do become challenging, they have more ability to respond in an appropriate way as they're not driven by negative emotions and are already in a good place mentally.

THE IMPORTANCE OF PLAY

There are numerous scientific studies regarding having fun and the positive impact this has on kids.

There is also research that suggests being deprived of play as a child has a negative impact on psychological wellbeing as people move into adulthood.

Play and having fun isn't only essential for kids, it's essential for adults too. There have been various studies around the positive impact of play and having fun for adults. They include:

- Reducing stress
- Improved ability to cope
- Boosting energy
- Improving memory and concentration
- Improving our ability to connect with others
- Better-quality sleep and getting to sleep more quickly
- Promoting positive patterns of behaviour.

If you're in a better place mentally and emotionally, then your quality of life is going to be better. People are naturally drawn to people who are enjoyable to be around.

SPONTANEITY IS KEY

Research suggests that it's undirected fun that lights up what's known as the pleasure centre in the brain. That means it's not just about doing fun things, but about doing things that bring you joy spontaneously.

It might be singing in the morning or waving to a bus full of people. Anything that on the spur of the moment makes you feel good.

It's about having fun just because it's fun, no other reason.

Now Your Turn: Find your fun

On a scale of one to 10, with 10 being the most fun you could have, what would be your current fun score for your life?

If you've scored yourself seven or above, you're doing pretty well. If it's five or below, you need to find ways to increase the fun in your life.

Ask yourself what you really enjoy and have fun doing, and build those into your week. If you wait for the 'right' time they'll never happen, you have to build them into your week and make them happen. You will find the full version of this exercise at www.be-more-kid.com.

FUN VS. ENJOYMENT

It's important to make the distinction between fun and enjoyment. Enjoying something isn't the same as having fun.

Having fun is about that feeling of child-like joy when you do something. It's spontaneous, it makes you laugh. It makes you joyful.

Ask yourself whether you're enjoying what you're doing or whether you're having fun. If you're just enjoying things, find a way to introduce some more fun into your life.

When you watch kids having fun, they seem full of joy. The moment of feeling joy is an intense emotion. It makes you want to jump up and down, you can't help but smile and laugh.

That's the feeling of joy you want to tap into. As an adult, you have to remember that kids find these moments of joy in everything from splashing in a swimming pool or blowing bubbles to having an ice cream or making balloon animals.

The sweet spot is reaching that point where you genuinely don't care what other people think of you. It could be as simple as wearing colourful clothes or pointy boots, like Ed does.

It's about getting to the point that you're totally at ease with who you are and completely engaged with whatever you're doing at that moment, so that nothing else seems to matter.

HOW TO FIND YOUR FUN

Do things because they're fun and joyful and for no other reason. Don't worry about what other people might think about you. Just focus on finding that joy in your daily life.

Find a way to make the tasks that you don't enjoy more fun. This is a really easy way to bring more fun into your life.

If you've got a boring journey to work, listen to an audiobook or your favourite music. If you've got to do the washing up or cooking, you could put the radio on or phone someone you want to talk to whilst you do it.

You're still doing the thing that you need to do, but you're finding a way to make it more fun. That might mean buying yourself flowers, or taking a different route to work that's more scenic.

Turn tasks into a game. Think about how everything becomes a game for kids. As a parent, making a task into a game is a great way to get your kids to engage with it.

Ed's story

One of my first part-time jobs as a student was working on the checkout at Tesco. To this day, it's one of the most fun jobs I've ever had.

That's because I was with a group of like-minded people and we turned things into a game. For example, if any customer wanted to put an item back, we'd throw it around between us. If you were on the checkout, you'd throw it to the person in charge of the checkout, who would then throw it to another member of staff and so on until it was back on the shelf.

We made a mundane task fun. We were enjoying it and the people in the shop were enjoying it. There's no reason why you can't do that with almost any task.

Ask yourself this question every day, 'Have I had fun today?' Check in with yourself around the middle of the day with that question and if the answer is 'No', how can you change it?

WHAT'S STOPPING YOU FROM HAVING FUN?

If you're not having fun, you have to think about why. For some people it will be because they feel guilty. There's a mental barrier that stops them from doing something like skipping down the street.

Or they'll start to do something and then stop themselves because they worry that they're too old, for instance.

As we become adults, life can become very serious. It can sometimes seem that you lurch from one crisis to another. That means your focus gets skewed and you start to focus on the things that are going wrong, rather than seeing the rest of your life, which actually may be going rather well.

For other people, they feel self-conscious when they're having fun. They worry about what other people will think and that holds them back.

If you've ever been on one of the amphibious vehicles, called a duck boat, you might have noticed that when you pass another duck everyone waves and you blow your 'quackers' to make a duck sound. It's part of this shared experience.

But if you were travelling by train, you wouldn't dream of waving to someone on a passing train. Ask yourself why not? It's those kinds of spontaneous things that are fun to do and it's what kids do, so it must be good!

If you start to adopt the things we're talking about in this book, you'll see a change in yourself but so will other people. Some of the people around you might think you're behaving strangely, or even tell you that you're being weird.

But you have to break out of that kind of thinking. If you get to the point where you're genuinely so in touch with who you are that you're present, playing games, having fun, finding joy and being your best self, some of the people around you will find that uncomfortable.

Just be brave enough to continue to be who you are or who you want to be.

BE MORE KID

Kids find joy in small acts. Waving at trains, blowing bubbles, jumping in puddles. As adults, we need to tap into that ability to find small moments of joy in our lives.

We need to do things because they're fun and for no other reason. The opportunities for this are endless, you just need to be conscious about it.

We appreciate that there are some things and situations that, for various reasons, it's less easy to change. That's what we're going to talk about in the next chapter: It's right for right now.

CHAPTER 17

IT'S RIGHT FOR RIGHT NOW

A s we've already said, kids think about what they want to do right now and they do it. Often as adults we know what we want to do but we say things like, 'I shouldn't …' or 'I couldn't …' or 'I'd better not …'

Have you ever wanted to get up and sing karaoke, but something stops you? What is it that actually stops you? Only you!

This chapter is all about reconnecting with your authentic self, what we also refer to as the unconscious mind. It's about utilising our experience as an adult with the characteristics we had as kids to get the best of both worlds.

People often try to think too far ahead and get lost in overwhelm. They get caught up in looking for what they should be doing in life. Instead you need to go with the flow, enjoy the journey and see where it takes you.

It's right for right now.

WAITING FOR INSPIRATION

Have you ever wondered what you're going to do with your life? When you look at everyone else, do they all seem to have it sorted?

Nicky's story

This is what I used to think. I used to look around and feel as though everyone else I knew had their lives together and I just didn't know what I was going to do with my life.

When I look back at this now, I don't know what I was expecting to happen. Did I think that I'd suddenly have some kind of flash of inspiration, like a bolt of lightning, when suddenly I'd know what I wanted to do with the rest of my life?

I could do the easy part. I knew what I *didn't* want to do. But how could I turn that around and find out what I wanted to do? I used to wonder, 'How do people know that?'

When I look back on my dilemma, I realise that my thinking was flawed from the very beginning, because that's not the way it works. I was trying to see the destination without embarking on the journey.

For many people, part of the issue stems from the fact that they're looking for what they want to be. Often this is programmed from when we're young because we get asked the question, 'What do you want to be when you grow up?'

That sets us on the path of believing there's an end destination we should be aiming for. When it changes to, 'What would you like to do?' that's a completely different mindset because there are many, many different paths that you could take.

For a lot of people, the next question that pops up is, 'What if I take the wrong path?'

This fear of following the 'wrong' path keeps people stuck. When they can't decide what the end destination is, they're fearful of making the wrong decision. That means they don't make any decision at all and they stay where they are.

They wait for a sign to help them decide and allow them to move forward. But when you do set off on the 'right' path and an obstacle appears, you start to question whether this was the right path after all.

Maybe that obstacle is a sign that you're making a mistake. This leads to more doubt, more indecision and, once again, you're stuck.

THERE IS NO 'WRONG' PATH

What if we told you that there is no 'wrong' path? How would that sound? What would you do if you knew you couldn't fail?

From where we're looking at it, every experience provides you with new resources. These are the resources you'll draw on and will then influence the next step on your journey.

As you gather those resources on your journey, they may change the direction your journey takes. What you have to remember is that you need to make the journey to gather the resources. Otherwise you'll remain stuck in the tunnel, unable to see the light at the other end.

If you attempt to see the destination from the wrong side of the tunnel, you're setting yourself up to fail. If you're waiting for the tunnel to disappear and a destination to come to you, then you'll be waiting forever.

You've got to experience life to live life, because you can't live life without experience.

A lot of people get hung up on the idea that they'll waste a lot of time if they make the wrong decision. But to actually live a life you've got to have experiences, that's the only way to do it.

This is about knowing and getting comfortable with the idea that you're on a journey where there is no right or wrong route.

The route you take is perfect for that moment in time. And while it may not get you an outcome, you need to understand that you're continually changing as a person as you go through life and gain more experience.

Often as people get older their priorities change. The things that satisfied them when they were younger don't satisfy them when they're older.

It's about recognising that and just living life, and living it to the full.

If you bring this back to the idea of life being like a train journey, where there is light at the end of the tunnel that's not another train, the next station is just one of many on that route.

You can get off at that station if you want, if you like what you see. And if not, you can hop back on and travel to the next station. If we adopt this mindset then it gives us permission to take opportunities, understanding that whatever decisions we make are right for right now.

This takes the pressure off, and stops you searching for an ultimate destination. You may find something that you want to do for the rest of your life, but equally you may continue to experience and explore.

MAKE SURE YOU'RE MOVING FORWARD

There's a difference between moving forward and choosing to change direction as you learn and grow, and not making a decision at all.

There's also a difference between genuinely moving forward and setting off but flip-flopping backwards and forwards and becoming paralysed because of indecision about making the right choice.

This is about moving forward and being okay with that. As you're moving forward, you're gathering those experiences and choosing to take the next experience, even though you don't know what that is because you can't see it from where you are.

YOU ONLY FAIL IF YOU GIVE UP

Experiences, good and bad, are all part of the journey. When things seem tough they're laying the groundwork for what's to come. It's a journey that doesn't stop.

The only time you'll fail is if you give up. It's a bit like Thomas Edison and the light bulb. He didn't fail, he just found 10,000 ways that didn't work before he found the one that did.

That's the way you have to treat life, and the frame you have to hold it in. The reason you fail when you give up is because you'll never know where that could have led to.

Instead you have to accept that the decision you've made in the moment is the best decision for you at that time. Hindsight is a perfect science and it's easy to berate ourselves for what looks like a stupid mistake, but at the time it was the perfect place for you to be in your life.

The main thing is to learn from it. Remember that saying from your mum, 'It's not what happened, it's what happens next that matters'.

DON'T BOX YOURSELF IN

Adults often want to fit everything into a box. We've been programmed by questions like, 'What do you want to be when you grow up?'

But as soon as we get that box, we try to fit everything in our lives into it. The trouble is, for a lot of adults that box becomes a prison.

They get stuck in that imaginary box with limited beliefs, which become bars and then they can't get out. Eventually they forget that there's anything outside of that box.

Life becomes repetitive and stuck. It's the same life, different day. To break free of this box, people need to start having experiences again. They need to start experiencing the journey and put the awe back into life.

It's only by doing this that you'll see the opportunities and get fulfilled by this notion of creativity and excitement.

HOW TO MAKE CHANGES

We coach a lot of people who have problems because they don't know who they want to be. They reach a certain age and feel as though they should have found it by now.

What you have to remember is that some changes take time. This is something we tell a lot of people who are training with us to become coaches themselves.

Many of them want to coach as a full-time business, but doing that successfully means they need to transition from their current full-time occupation.

Although there are some schools of thought that you should just take the leap, because that will force you. A 'There's no going back' kind of attitude, that's not something we advocate.

In our experience, the people who jump without the foundations in place for success experience huge amounts of stress and become worried about how they're going to pay their bills.

They become so worried about this, that their focus goes. As a result, they often lose sight of their business plan, if they even had one in the first place.

What they start doing then is jumping at any opportunity to make an income, which can often be way off their original plan and outside of their area of expertise. That can lead them into difficult situations.

You have to remember that even when you're living your best life, there will always be tough things that you need to do and that you would prefer not to do. But it's about recognising that those things play an important part in the bigger picture.

Some people will think that they've failed if, whilst they are developing their new business, they have to work doing the job they don't want, to give them the income they need to put food on the table and a roof over their heads. But as long as you're moving forward, you haven't failed.

You have to do what you need to do, and that means accepting things are right for right now.

YOU ALWAYS KNOW THE RIGHT THING TO DO

Often you already know the right thing to do, you just don't pay attention to it. People will go off on a retreat or they'll travel around the world trying to find themselves.

But actually, if you listen, stop and pay attention then you'll realise your unconscious mind is telling you what to do and you're just ignoring it. You're looking externally for the right answer instead of paying attention to what's going on internally. Once you're aware of what you need to do, you need to take the right action to make it happen. Many people make a decision but then don't take action.

The other thing to remember is that you always have to solve a problem in the place in which it was created.

You'll often see examples of how not to handle this in workplaces, where one person puts in complaints or grievances and then gets moved to a different department and the whole thing happens again.

In this example, the organisation needs to solve the issue with that specific employee, otherwise the pattern of behaviour just repeats.

This can be the problem with taking yourself away from your daily life to find the solutions to your problems: you won't deal with what created them. You can be contemplating everything in Bali and it will all feel fine, but then you'll return home and you'll be right back where you started.

You have to be in the environment where the problem is to be able to find the solution. If you don't do that, you'll just keep dragging your problems with you through life.

RIGHT FOR RIGHT NOW

Nicky's story

When I was working in the Civil Service, I always had my eye on the next promotion, because it was important to me that I got to a certain grade. That's where my focus was.

But when I decided to have my girls, I took a year out and then I went back part-time. On the one hand, I knew that wasn't going to get me where I needed to be professionally. But on the other hand, it was right for right then.

That was my decision. I didn't want to put my career on hold indefinitely, so I made sure that there were things in place so I could focus on my career again as soon as they reached a certain age.

I knew it would be win–win. And sure enough, I had my time out when the girls were young, then I put my plan into action when the time was right and I started to get promotions again.

It's about being aware and conscious that you're not always going to get everything that you need as quickly as you'd like it. The key is knowing that you're still moving forward and appreciating that this decision is right for right now.

BE YOU

You need to be in touch with who you are because your life will reflect the choices you make. If you're always trying to create an impression of who you are that's not true to you, you'll attract the type of people who are fulfilling that impression, not the real you.

As soon as you're honest about who you are, everything seems to get easier. You'll attract the people who are supposed to be in your life. It all starts with you.

When you own your truth and who you are, everything around you starts to change and that's where the joy comes from.

If you're not true to yourself, you'll cause all kinds of issues for yourself further down the line. Own who you are, be who you are and be happy with who you are.

BE MORE KID

Kids don't plan ahead. They do what they do in the moment and they enjoy it. Adults often give themselves a hard time because they get too caught up in their own thoughts and self-talk.

They worry too much about what they think they should be doing. They give themselves a hard time for not living up to their (often unrealistic) expectations.

By being more kid, life will become much easier and more enriching. You'll enjoy each experience along your journey and you'll be amazed at the opportunities that present themselves.

It's all because once you start thinking in that way, you'll see things that you wouldn't have seen before.

In the next part of the book we'll be tapping back into the resources you had easy access to as a kid and rediscovering the Art & Science of Underthinking.

Part VI

The Art & Science of Underthinking

When was the last time you woke up at the start of the day and felt excited?

When you were a kid, chances are every day was like that. It was a blank canvas full of fun and opportunities. The only thing that's changed is your mindset and the Art & Science of Underthinking.

Think back to when you were a kid. Visualise a specific time when you wanted to go to bed earlier so the big day would arrive quicker. Except when you got into bed, you were far too excited to sleep!

But somehow, sleep crept up on you, and when you opened your eyes it was TODAY and you could hardly contain yourself with the excitement of it all. You were so excited you couldn't eat or sit still. Do you remember at least one time like that in your life?

Looking back on that as an adult, that much excitement can seem a bit uncomfortable, overwhelming even. As we grow older, this innocent and pure joy at life is all too often replaced by cynicism and negativity.

The things that we once viewed with awe we can easily take for granted and we become complacent about them.

Throughout our research we have discovered that one of the most useful traits kids have, which gives them this ability to live life to the full, is the skill of underthinking.

But from the adult world, which often revolves around overthinking, how do we regain the ability to underthink? In this part of the book we're looking at the Art & Science of Underthinking and the four principles behind it that will help us all to Be More Kid!

CHAPTER 18

KEEPING IT SIMPLE

If you ask kids why they are doing something they will say simply because they want to. There's no convoluted reason as to how it fits in with something else. There's no huge explanation or justification, as an adult would give.

They are simply doing it because they want to. We can learn from that.

When we asked one of the kids we interviewed what their favourite game was, they told us it was 'tig' because they got to run around a lot. How fantastic is that?

What we can learn from this is to keep things simple. That's the first principle that will help you tap into the Art & Science of Underthinking and it's one that brings many benefits.

As adults we become really good at doing things we don't want to do, instead of the things we do want to do.

As we mentioned earlier, we know there are things that must be done. But hopefully you've already picked up some ideas to make them more fun, or at least accept that they're right for right now.

Let's look at how we can simplify the rest.

WHY DO YOU ENJOY BEING ON HOLIDAY?

There's a question for you. We're sure if you live in the UK that better weather abroad will play a part. But think more deeply about what it is about being on holiday that you enjoy. Why do you feel so much more refreshed and relaxed when you come back than you did when you set off?

We can tell you the reason. It's because the stresses and strains of life are removed from your environment. You have little to think about except what you should eat next from the all-inclusive buffet and whether you have enough suntan lotion to last you the rest of your break.

Life on holiday becomes extremely simple and you give yourself permission to have fun and enjoy yourself.

As the plane lands back in your home country, you'll often hear mumblings of, 'back to the real world' or 'back to the grind'.

At least one travel company has taken the opportunity to tap into this melancholy by giving out holiday brochures on the return journey. They offer a really low deposit for people to book their next break so they can look forward to escaping their lives again.

Surely there must be more to life than this series of highs and lows? How much better would it be if we looked forward to coming home and enjoyed daily life as much as we look forward to being away?

WHY DO PEOPLE LONG TO ESCAPE?

One of the reasons adults feel so stressed and long to escape is because of the demands they place on their time. This isn't about time management, there will always be 24 hours in a day.

This is about the attempt to fit more tasks into those 24 hours than you have the ability to complete comfortably.

Then there are the financial strains and the cycle of buying bigger and better, which we've mentioned earlier in the book. This means you need more finances, until it seems there's no way out. Often this results in you working even harder and longer hours in a job you don't enjoy.

HOW DO YOU START TO RECTIFY THIS AND REDRESS THE BALANCE?

Now Your Turn: Where can you make life more simple?

Begin by looking at time. We've already spoken about how you can free up time to do the things that are important to you.

This exercise will take that one step further to help you identify where in your life you're overcomplicating things and missing the opportunity to keep things simple.

Time

Start by taking yourself through your daily routine for the next seven days. Write down all the tasks you need to complete, all the places you need to be and write down timings next to each one for each day.

This will allow you to see exactly what you spend your days doing. When you do this in advance, it can appear that you should have a lot of space in your day. You might start to wonder where the time disappears to.

Put those notes to one side. The second part of this exercise is to record the actual time it takes to do all those tasks and make those journeys, as well as anything else you didn't account for.

This can be quite laborious if you do it for every single thing you do in a day, so restrict it to summarising every hour of how you spent your time. This will give you enough information to see how you're really spending your time.

At the end of the seven days, ask yourself the following question for each of the tasks you did or journeys you made: Was this really necessary?

If the answer is 'Yes', ask yourself this question: Could I have done that in a different way that would have made life easier and more simple?

This is an opportunity to lift yourself out of autopilot mode and identify exactly how you can simplify your life.

(continued)

Here are a few things to think about when you review your list:

- Do you need to take your car everywhere or could you walk instead? Walking gives you an opportunity to slow your life down and notice what's going on around you.
- Do you need to make so many trips to the store? Would life be simpler if you did your shopping online and had it delivered?
- Is it possible to work from home once or twice a week? Have you ever asked your employer this question, or thought about how much time you would save by not having to commute to work?
- If you have a stressful job that you don't like, have you considered reducing your hours?
- Do you need to restrict time on social media or watching TV?

Money

As well as assessing how you spend your time, you should also assess how you spend your money. When was the last time you assessed how much it costs you to be at work?

If you're in a job that you don't like and that causes you stress, would you be better off taking a lower-paid role closer to home? Could you reduce your hours?

This may not have as much of a financial impact as you imagine, especially when you take into account travelling and parking costs, as well as childcare expenses. You may also pay less tax.

When you look into the differences in your finances, understand that this is the price of simplifying your life. How much is it worth to you? Where can you make savings?

Do you really need the expensive TV subscription? And if you didn't have it, what could you do with your time instead that would be more fun and educational?

The opportunities really are endless. It's your life, you owe it to yourself to enjoy it. You will find the full version of this exercise at www.be-more-kid.com.

AUDIT YOUR LIFE

Life gets cluttered. People often say they haven't got time to enjoy themselves or to relax, but the truth is that they're not using their time effectively. Carrying out these exercises, along with ones like the Wheel of Life that we mentioned earlier in the book, will help you check in.

You need to audit your life regularly. We recommend doing it at least once a year to find the areas where you can simplify and declutter.

Mark's story

Some years ago a woman who was on one of our training courses came to me and said that she wanted to go full-time with her hypnotherapy business, but that she didn't have time.

I gave her one simple piece of advice, 'Get rid of your TV'. I'm sure she told me that she didn't watch much TV anyway, but I insisted that this is the kind of thing that falls unconscious when it comes to how you're spending your time.

About a month later, she was on another of our courses. She approached me and said, 'I did what you suggested. It was brilliant'.

I asked her to remind me what I suggested, because I often forget. She said, 'Getting rid of the TV set. It was a great idea. Now we have special movie evenings with the kids where we all gather round my laptop screen with popcorn and watch a film'.

She just kept talking about all the benefits, 'I didn't realise it, but when the kids were coming home from school they were just putting the TV on. They were all getting drawn into it and they weren't doing their homework. Now they come home from school, do their homework and it's done. It's just a better environment'.

This demonstrates what that last exercise is trying to show you, that if you take stock of your life you can see where you expand tasks to fill time and change your behaviour to make it more efficient and productive.

ASK HOW YOU CAN USE TIME MORE EFFECTIVELY

You need to use this as an opportunity to find different ways of doing things to help you use your time more effectively. For example, if you have to make a long car journey, how can you use that time more effectively? Could you listen to an audiobook so that you're learning something?

Think about what you can prioritise to achieve in that time which frees you up when you get to work and allows you to work more efficiently.

The most important thing underlying all of this is that you can't manage your tasks effectively if you don't know how long they really take. It's easy to overestimate how long something will take, and then you expand the task to fill that time.

Nicky's story

Sometimes by challenging your assumptions the changes you make can surprise you.

In order to run our training business, I was mainly working from home and would only go into the office for meetings or to catch up with people. I thought that if I worked in the office full-time, I wouldn't get all of my work done due to distractions.

The problem was that my work tasks were spilling over into the evenings and weekends. I decided to change my routine for a week, spending every day working from the office.

My initial thought was that I wouldn't get all of my work done, but to my amazement I became more efficient, got all of my tasks done and incorporated all those other things I used to go into the office for.

Now that means when I'm leaving the office I've finished my work for the day and I can enjoy my evenings. Sometimes doing things differently can help.

HOW TO ASSESS YOUR LIFE

There are some questions you should ask yourself if you want to manage your tasks more effectively, have more time and simplify your life.

Ask yourself these questions regularly:

- What are the things you need to do?
- What things do you need to stop doing?
- Where are you not getting value in your life?
- If you were looking to employ someone to get the most value out of your life, would you employ yourself?

BE MORE KID

Kids keep things simple. They're helped in keeping things simple by the structure that's imposed on them by their parents and at school.

They eat at set times, go to bed at set times, have a certain amount of time for play and watching TV. It's all very controlled.

When they go to school they have the timetable for their lessons and everything is blocked in for them. What you can take from this is that when life is organised and ordered and the right amount of time is allowed for the right things, life is more effective and efficient.

You have to control how much time you're spending on each of your tasks. Remove tasks that you don't need to do or don't enjoy doing as much as possible. Keep things simple.

CHAPTER 19

IT'S NOT PERSONAL

The second principle of the Art & Science of Underthinking that kids naturally adopt is that they don't take things personally.

What we mean by this is that they let things go. Think about it. When a kid is told they must do something, or the opposite – that they can't do something – they may complain and sulk in the moment but it only takes a tiny distraction for them to forget all about it.

They certainly don't hold onto what has happened once it's over and done with. This is true even when they think their friends aren't playing fair, or that they're being left out.

Both of these situations are the main areas of contention for kids, but still they return to business as usual as soon as the situation changes or it's forgotten.

Compare this to how adults deal with things. When something happens, they hold onto it, sometimes for a lifetime. We know of families where some family members haven't spoken for decades over something which, in the greater scheme of things, was a trivial comment or situation at the time.

You also see this all the time in the workplace. If someone isn't progressing as well or as quickly as they believe they should, they often blame their boss for not giving them the credit that they think they deserve.

Or when they see other people doing better than them, they'll believe it's because they're getting favourable treatment from their boss.

The problem is that once you have this belief, the chances of being able to turn it around with that individual are remote because, whether it's accurate or not, in your model of the world it's true.

As a result, how you react to your boss will be unconsciously influenced by your belief that your boss doesn't like you. Before the situation becomes uncomfortable, why not see it as a kid would ...

WHAT WOULD A KID DO?

In our research with kids, we asked them what someone should do if there were people who weren't being very nice to them and it was making them unhappy. They replied that they should go somewhere else and be with people who are going to be nice to them. In the eyes of a kid, it is really very simple.

You may be thinking to yourself that it's not as simple as that and, of course, we appreciate that in adult life there may be other considerations to take into account. But you have to ask yourself, if things aren't working out where you are how bad does it have to get before you do something about it?

Remember that if you're not the driver in your life then you're the passenger. If someone else is doing the driving, you are not in control.

You also have to remember that we are only able to interpret things through our own model of the world. We can never really know what someone's intention is for carrying out particular behaviour. Any mind reads that we do are only based on how we perceive that behaviour.

Wouldn't life be much more pleasant if we adopted the mindset that all interactions are carried out from a place of best intention or, in other words, that this person has our best outcome at heart.

Whether that is actually true or not is irrelevant, because if we adopt that mindset then we're not influenced by what we think someone's saying behind the scenes.

Adults often place limitations on what they say and do because of what they think someone else might think. You hear people saying things like, 'I can't go there because so-and-so won't be happy', or 'If I talk to them I'll upset so-and-so'.

But if the people around you are really behaving in that way and it's having an adverse impact on your life then there's always a choice. It may be a less-easy choice, but in our eyes short-term discomfort is always a better option than being in an unpleasant situation in the long term.

HOW DO YOU ADOPT THE MINDSET OF IT NOT BEING PERSONAL?

It's about catching yourself in the moment. Noticing when you think things like, 'They've never liked me', or 'They're doing that on purpose to annoy me'.

We all have different personality traits and chances are that you just have different communication styles. If that's the case, then you are as much responsible for your communication as they are for theirs. If it's important then forget about taking it personally and find a way to make it work.

Carl Jung, the Swiss psychologist, has an interesting theory that's worth considering at this point. He said that if you're feeling negative emotions around what someone else is saying or doing, that's because it is behaviour that you are capable of carrying out yourself and that you are in denial about.

According to Carl Jung, the more negative emotion you feel, the more it is like you and the more outside of your awareness it is. This can be a hard pill to swallow and it's often much easier to blame other people.

Yet, if you want to become the master of your emotions then it's good to notice where your challenges are and be conscious about where in your life you might actually be carrying out the same behaviour, that you haven't previously noticed.

RESPOND, DON'T REACT

The problem is that most people react rather than responding. They react based on emotional triggers that are outside their conscious awareness.

What you want to learn to do is to respond. That involves stepping back for a moment and really embracing this idea that you have total control over how you feel, that no-one can make you feel a certain way.

If you believe someone else has power over your feelings, you're disempowering yourself. This comes back to what we discussed in Chapter 4, about being a passenger or being a driver.

THE WORLD IS A MIRROR

Another way to think of Carl Jung's theory is that the world is a mirror and it reflects all of your imperfections, as well as your good qualities.

We're sure you've heard the phrase, 'When you point the finger there are three pointing back at you'. This idea also applies here too.

For example, at work there are often one or two people who are considered to be the office gossips. But how often have you heard someone saying, 'So-and-so is a terrible gossip, if only you heard what she says around the water cooler. Oh, by the way, did you hear that so-and-so in accounts has been having an affair with so-and-so in admin ...' They're carrying out the behaviour that they're complaining about someone else doing and they don't even realise they're doing it.

How do you bring that into your awareness and stop yourself from doing it? When you go to point the finger, stop and think about the other three fingers pointing back at you.

Carl Jung says that you can only develop as a person by bringing more of what he calls your shadow self into your conscious awareness. So when you think about those fingers pointing back at you, ask yourself these questions:

- Is this somewhere I need to develop?
- Is it informational feedback for me?
- Is that why I don't like it and am taking it personally at an unconscious level?

When you recognise that, you can stop and realise you have a choice in how you feel, and why should you give away your power to someone else?

WHAT COULD YOU LEARN?

People often give unsolicited feedback. You can choose to ignore it, but if you're completely closed to it you might be missing an opportunity to learn something that could be of benefit to you.

Sometimes people do take feedback personally because they feel it's questioning their abilities, skills, capabilities or who they are as a person. Often that means they reject it instantly without exploring whether there's anything they could learn.

If, on the other hand, you treat it as information and don't take it personally, there might be something of use to you in there.

You have to look at it from the perspective that we can only ever get better by getting feedback off people. Always appreciate the feedback you're given, but know that it's your choice what you do with it.

REVERTING TO DEFAULT PROGRAMMING

One of the things that we've talked about a lot is the idea that you're re-programming your mind.

But it's worth bearing in mind that, whenever people are under stress they revert to their default programming. You've therefore got to hardwire any changes you make into your neurology, because when the chips are down you'll revert to your neurological response.

You have to think of this as a constant evolution to set up a new version of yourself. Because the thing is, people can personally develop but not change neurologically, not change their hardwired responses. But it's those hardwired responses that will come out when you're under stress.

ACCEPT WHAT YOU'RE CAPABLE OF

People don't always like the notion of what they're capable of. For example, people often have very strong emotions around people murdering other people. They say things like, 'I think that's wrong' and 'I would never do that'.

But if they have kids and we ask what they'd do if someone sexually assaulted their kid, the response is often, 'I'd kill them'.

These are emotions that are buried deep inside, they're not conscious. But the more you dig into these things the more you have to accept what you're capable of. You need to accept that in those circumstances, for example, you'd be capable of murdering someone. That's an extreme example, but what happens when you start to accept those things within yourself is that you stop getting upset about other people exhibiting that behaviour. We are not saying that you are agreeing with or condoning the behaviour, it is simply about looking to take the emotional reactive charge off things.

If you accept that you can gossip too, then why get upset when other people do it?

We've said the world is a mirror reflecting back at you, but this is about not being upset by what you see in that reflection, not having that emotional reaction so that you can respond.

BE MORE KID

Kids are incredibly accepting. They accept and get on with anyone. They don't think anything is a problem or an issue. Imagine how great it would feel if you could just accept the things you don't like in other people. Think about how little stress you'd have.

We've mentioned already how we develop as kids and it's noticeable that young children will accept everyone until they're programmed not to. So, to be more kid, just let things go, because that's what kids do. They don't hold onto things. They're just in the moment and then they move on.

The next time you start to feel upset or angry about something, ask yourself, 'Will this matter in six months' time?' If the answer is No', then just forget about it.

What's the point in creating unpleasant situations and disagreements over things that just don't matter?

CHAPTER 20

BE EXCITED

The third principle of the Art & Science of Underthinking is something that kids do really easily and on a regular basis: be excited.

As we mentioned at the beginning of this part of the book, can you remember at least one time when you were young when you were so excited you could barely sit still? When you were waiting for these things, time seemed to drag forever. Sometimes it would even stop you sleeping.

When you look back, there are a number of events that prompt this level of excitement: Christmas Eve, the day before your birthday, the day before you go on holiday.

But we're sure there were also times when you got really excited, just not on quite such a mammoth scale.

It could be a day at school, when you got to play pirates instead of doing maths. Or when you were expecting a new outfit to be delivered from a catalogue.

Looking back on those events decades later, can you still feel the excitement you felt then? We can. Yet, as an adult, we become complacent about things that we would have felt so excited about in the past.

What made these things so exciting as a kid and why does that fade as we get older?

EXCITEMENT COMES FROM MEANING

Thinking back, the excitement often wasn't about the event itself, but about the meaning given to that event or what went with the event.

For example, birthdays meant getting surprise presents, having birthday tea, knowing you could eat as much as you wanted and even get away with having more than one cake. Probably most of all, they were about feeling special.

This is especially true if you have siblings. It's not that you don't feel special all the time, but that on your birthday you can justify putting your needs and wants first. It's a day when everything doesn't have to be equal and shared.

The excitement you feel as a kid that occurred on more of an everyday basis was based on doing things that were enjoyable, spending time with people you really liked or cared about, going to places that were fun, or just doing something a little out of the ordinary.

This is also what we found in the research we did with kids. They were really excited when they were about to do something or go somewhere that they thought was going to be really enjoyable and fun.

WHY DO WE LOSE OUR EXCITEMENT FOR LIFE?

Even though we might do these things as an adult, and we plan to do them because we believe we're going to enjoy them, we don't get the same feeling of excitement that we did when we were kids.

There are several reasons for this.

PROGRAMMING

What reaction did you get when you became overexcited as a kid? You were probably told to calm down, sit still and stop jumping around.

Kids want to please and be liked, so they start to find strategies to be able to behave in a more socially acceptable way. One method of managing this is to not think about the things you're excited about.

When you're really young, parents actually draw out excitement in kids and encourage it. They want them to be excited about going for a walk, playing with a new toy, having a friend over to play.

But as you get older, parents start to suppress it because they don't want their kids to be over the top. When you go to school, that just continues. You have to follow the rules of what you can and can't do. You're programmed not to show your excitement and often that means you don't feel excited in the same way.

'UNCOOL' TO SHOW EMOTION

As you develop through childhood, it becomes uncool to show that you're excited about something, especially around your peer group.

Showing any emotion at all can leave you feeling vulnerable, so it's safer not to show that you actually care.

DON'T FEEL IN CONTROL OF YOUR EMOTIONS

Some people don't like feeling emotions because they don't feel in control. They learn to distance themselves from their feelings and that means that not only do they not feel excitement, they don't feel anything at all.

When this has gone on for some time, they can lose the ability to experience any real emotions. They might worry about embarrassing themselves or feel as though experiencing emotions is like opening Pandora's box. They're concerned that if they do that, the whole structure of their life will come tumbling down.

FEAR OF DISAPPOINTMENT

Massive highs are often followed by equally massive lows. If you're really looking forward to something and then it doesn't happen for whatever reason, you feel terrible.

When that happens, it makes it easier to not look forward to anything until it actually happens. But by the time it does happen you are already there and in the experience, so you lose the build-up which is when you'd usually feel the excitement.

DON'T FEEL LIKE THERE'S ANYTHING TO BE EXCITED ABOUT

This is the main reason why adults don't get excited. Everyday life is boring, they may not enjoy their job and they're tired. That makes doing something out of the ordinary seem like more effort than they feel they have the energy for.

It becomes a self-fulfilling prophecy, because they never feel they have the energy to do something different. So they just continue as they are.

But what they don't realise is that doing something different would break the cycle. It's no wonder that people get depressed when they feel trapped in a life that doesn't give them any happiness. They can't see the light at the end of the tunnel.

Adults procrastinate, especially over things they don't like doing. But that stops them getting excited about what that task might lead to. Without the excitement, they lack the motivation and continue to procrastinate.

WHY SHOULD YOU BE EXCITED?

The first reason we're suggesting you should be excited is because it's one of the four principles of the Art & Science of Underthinking.

Being excited is a powerful positive emotion. When you feel it, your body releases a host of happy hormones: dopamine, endorphins, serotonin and oxytocin. It changes your brain on a chemical level. Being excited is motivating, and that leads us to take action because we want to feel that way again.

Feeling excited is what happens when you connect with your purpose. If you have a purpose and it's singing to you, you're going to want to do things in connection with that purpose. This is a natural process that happens when we are living our purpose. We automatically feel excited about doing something that we want to do.

When you connect with your purpose, you can find the motivation for the mundane tasks that you don't like because you understand how that connects to your purpose, and that's exciting. Being excited is a way of reconnecting with your inner kid and experiencing the feeling of the sheer joy of being alive.

CONTROLLED EXCITEMENT

It's not quite true that adults don't feel excitement, but they do so in a very controlled way. Advertisers have become experts at creating excitement. They know how powerful this emotion is.

Think about when Apple release a new iPhone. There's always a big build-up to get the excitement going. It's even reached the point where they've timed how long it should take for you to open the box that your phone arrives in, in order for you to experience maximum excitement.

There's the suction as you open the box. Then you feel the weight as the phone drops out. All carefully researched and timed to perfection to create and deliver against maximum anticipation.

Advertisers will ramp up the excitement by leaking information about new products prior to their release. These are things you're allowed to get excited about as an adult.

What we want you to do is think about how to generate internal excitement, rather than requiring external things to get excited about. It comes back to the issue of control. Be in control of your excitement rather than being controlled and told what to be excited about.

HOW DO YOU BEGIN FEELING EXCITED AGAIN?

The first step is to actually have something to be excited about. If you're doing something you're passionate about you'll naturally feel excited as you look forward to doing the things that are important to you.

People who feel they have a purpose in life naturally get excited on a regular basis. If you don't feel that there's anything you're passionate about, go back to the exercise earlier in the book about finding your purpose. Once you discover your purpose and carry out activities to fulfil this, you'll feel excited again. That's because you've been inspired and will look forward to doing the things that are really important to you.

Think about Christmas. The Christmas adverts come on TV and we're 'allowed' to start getting excited about Christmas. But just pause for a moment and think about why you're excited for Christmas. Is it the food, or seeing the people you love? You could do that at any time of the year, you don't need Christmas for that. Excitement is like a puppy, it's for life, not just for Christmas.

If you take the essence of what you're excited about, you'll find that it's stuff you can do all the time. You just have to put it into your life.

Ask yourself, 'When was the last time you spent time with the people you love or whose company you enjoy and you feel good being with?' If you make doing the things that you enjoy a priority, you will get excited about them and your life will improve.

If you don't feel like you have the energy to break the cycle, the next chapter and the fourth principle of the Art & Science of Underthinking will help you – Play more.

BE MORE KID

Excitement for kids is organic, authentic and natural. They get excited about the small things and, as a result, have a joy for life.

There are far more opportunities for excitement in your daily life than you think, and if you can tap into being more excited the benefits will be massive.

CHAPTER 21

PLAY MORE

There have been many studies regarding the importance of play for both children and adults. Playfulness in adults is strongly related to emotional wellbeing. It reduces stress, promotes relaxation, increases creativity, boosts imagination and enhances problem-solving abilities.

Somewhere between childhood and becoming an adult, play stops. Life becomes busier and more serious, we stop making time for play. When play stops, so do the benefits we get from play.

There are times when the urge to play can present itself, but this impulse is often dismissed because as adults we feel it isn't appropriate behaviour and are concerned about what other people will think of us. It's only when you become parents or grandparents that it's once again acceptable for you to join in the games, and both the children and the adults benefit.

WHY IS PLAY IMPORTANT?

Play is an important component in the Art & Science of Underthinking because, at the very least, it acts as a pattern interrupt.

It breaks the cycle where you're lacking in energy to lift yourself out of your daily life. In doing so it helps you relax and have fun. When you do that, you feel energised and connected with the people around you, with all of the additional benefits this brings.

Spontaneous play is particularly important, and research has shown that this gets the best results. This is about seizing the moment and doing what you feel like doing in that moment in time, because that's going to be more beneficial for you and those around you.

LIVING IN THE MOMENT

Kids find it really easy to get lost in the moment. You'll know this if you've ever been in a hurry and had a young child with you. It's impossible to go at anything other than a snail's pace.

Every step they take has something which absorbs their attention: a crack in the pavement with a plant growing out of it; metal railings that make a sound when they run their fingers over them; an insect on a wall; the dog in the neighbour's garden; stamping in a puddle – the list can go on and on.

Kids can literally spend hours examining and re-examining the same thing. While we're not suggesting we replicate this as an adult, just think about how much kids live in the moment. They're not concerned about where they're going or what's coming next, often much to the frustration of the adult who's trying to herd them along.

If we could reconnect with even just a small portion of this ability that we once had – to become absorbed in the moment, forget about everything else and just enjoy what we were doing at that time – think about how beneficial and restful that would be for our busy minds. It will allow them to switch off. That will produce positive levels of contentment and wellbeing.

BUILDING RELATIONSHIPS

Kids learn how to build relationships through play. They test different ways of doing things. And they watch the reactions they get from others. It's the same with adults. Play can also help us to defuse tricky situations. When people are having fun and feel relaxed, they feel safe to be themselves. That allows you to build new relationships, as well as to enhance and revitalise existing relationships, which benefits everyone.

You'll probably have heard the saying, 'Find a job you love and you'll never work a day in your life'. It's an ethos that more and more companies are taking onboard. Companies are including play, or a playful environment, as part of their culture. Why? Because it brings benefits to the business.

Given that studies show that play aids creativity and imagination, it's a great idea to encourage this as much as possible where the job role calls for it. Who says you can't have fun while you're working?

Happiness and contentment bring a host of health benefits to individuals. But put this in a work context and you see similar benefits. If someone wants to be at work because they enjoy it, they'll have great relationships with their colleagues. Absenteeism will naturally go down. A person who is well and happy is going to be more focused and motivated.

WHAT IS PLAY?

Now that we've explained why you should play more, we're going to look at how you can do that. But it helps to begin by defining what we mean by play. A dictionary definition that we like is, 'To engage in activity for enjoyment and recreation rather than a serious or practical purpose'.

In other words, to do something that you enjoy just because you want to.

What kinds of activity are play? That depends on the individual, as everyone has a different idea of what is enjoyable. Some people might think that running around in the rain is a great idea, especially if it's spontaneous. Someone else might think that under no circumstances would that be enjoyable.

You need to test out activities for yourself. Just give it a go, because you might enjoy something that you thought wasn't for you. Kids play all the time and it doesn't cost them anything. You certainly don't need to spend money to play.

If you need some ideas, look up free events in your town or city and you'll see plenty of opportunities that don't have to cost you anything. Workshops, outdoor pursuits, food festivals, music, walks, activities, it doesn't matter.

Find something that takes your fancy, commit to making it happen and do it. When you're there, put your phone away and fully engage, lose yourself in what you're doing. You will feel better for it.

Now Your Turn: Finding ways to play more

We suggest that you build into your days, a way to play every day for the next 14 days and make sure you do it, even if you feel tired or can't be bothered.

Here are some suggestions to get you started, but don't just stick to these ideas:

- Have a 'staycation' and visit places in your home town as though you've never been there before.
- Turn your TV off once or twice a week and play the board games you used to love as a kid.
- Try out a new sport or activity.
- Do a jigsaw.
- Play crazy golf.
- Take part in a group activity outdoors.
- Take a spontaneous road trip in the car. Pack a quick picnic to eat en-route, take an overnight bag and go where the road takes you.
- Get hold of some garden games, invite some friends and family round and get playing. If you don't have a garden, take the games to the park. Get everyone to bring an item of food and drink with them and see what arrives.
- Go to an amusement park and have fun on the rides.
- Take a trip to the seaside and visit an arcade. Do all the things you loved as a kid.
- Get a group of friends or family together and go ten-pin bowling. Make some prizes to give out or bring silly hats to wear when someone does something like getting a strike or missing all the pins completely. You will find the full version of this exercise at www.be-more-kid.com.

There's no end to the ideas you can come up with. The more you do this, the quicker and more easily the ideas will flow.

Nicky's story

For one of Mark's birthdays I gave him the choice of an activity from a list of suggestions. On the list were having dinner at a fancy restaurant, going to a concert, going to a place he'd never been before and axe-throwing.

Guess which one he chose? Axe-throwing of course!

We had a fantastic time. As much as we love food, it was much more fun to throw some axes around than to sit in a restaurant for a few hours. And it was cheaper too.

TIPS TO FIT MORE PLAY INTO YOUR LIFE

There are plenty of ways to fit more play into your life. The following are some tips, but see if you can find your own too.

In a corporate environment, you'll have a diary and all your meetings will go in there. Put an hour here and there a few times a week in your corporate diary and label it 'play'.

If you put it in there, you'll make time for it, just like you would for a meeting or a conference call. Then it's up to you to decide what that time involves.

It might be a sporting activity, going for a walk, doing an indoor skydive. It could be anything. We guarantee that once you start doing it and leave your corporate environment for an hour to play, you'll come back with a new sense of energy and purpose. You'll feel amazing.

The key is to schedule it though, because if you don't do this, it won't happen. If you're not in a position to schedule it in like a meeting, could you make your lunch break your play time?

You have to take personal responsibility to make it happen though. It's about reconnecting with that joy that comes from play and understanding that it's about having freedom. Our lives become so regimented, so introduce pockets of time to your day where you can be free and do what you want to do.

BE MORE KID

We all have the ability to play more within us, because we were all kids once. What we're asking you to do is reconnect with how you used to play when you were young. All too often as adults we're tied into the outcome or objective and we forget to enjoy the journey. We're racing from A to B to C and not stopping to see what there is along the way.

You restrict the having fun part until you get to your 'destination', whether that's the beach, the hotel for your holiday, the park, or wherever. Why not have fun on the journey too?

Mark and Nicky's story

On Sunday afternoons we meet up with the three hooligans, as Mark calls them (also known as our grandchildren). One place we like to go is Bradgate Park in Leicestershire.

It always starts with a walk from the car park to the tearoom. It's only about one mile, but it will take us hours to get there. It's like herding cats. One of the kids will be up a tree. Another one will be in a stream. The third one will be walking in cow poo. But they'll be enjoying themselves. They'll be playing and they don't care what's going on.

As an adult, it can be easy to get frustrated, because you're thinking about getting to the tearoom and are looking forward to eating cake. But think about everything you're missing along the way.

The kids remind you that there's so much to discover about the world along the way. They have so much curiosity. They experiment. As adults, we've lost that awe and wonder. We should be having fun on the journey, and the more spontaneous the better.

Your task from this part of the book is to find ways to play more.

By carrying out these four principles of keeping it simple, it's not personal, be excited and play more, you'll reconnect with the Art & Science of Underthinking, just as you did when you were a kid.

We guarantee you'll feel so much better for it.

CONCLUSION

The intention of this book is to reconnect you with your inner kid so you can regain that joy of life and feeling of inner contentment.

It's about identifying what happens as we grow into adults, and what gets in the way of us thinking the way we did when we were kids.

We want you to recognise the natural resources that kids have and reconnect with those resources as an adult, so you can live the life that you once imagined.

We've covered a lot in this book, so below is a brief summary of each of the chapters.

PART I-STUCK AND SETTLING FOR

WHY ARE YOU CHOOSING TO BE UNHAPPY?

Through our research we identified that people are not doing the things that are important to them. They're not having the relationships that they want.

They want to be accepted for who they are; be more positive; have more fun; make better choices and have a better life; as well as having a healthier lifestyle, including things like losing weight and having more money.

What stops them from having these things now? A number of things stop them from moving forward, including a lack of self-belief; feeling conflicted between doing something for themselves and what is right for their family and feeling guilty; not feeling positive and not trusting themselves.

The majority of people focus on all of the things that could possibly go wrong, resulting in anxiety and fear. This stops them from doing the things that they want to do. It's the biggest challenge they have to overcome.

In general, people are placing control for their lives and what they want to achieve in life in the hands of everyone else but themselves. As a result, they feel stuck and can't see a way forward.

They have lots of things that they want to do and they used to have dreams and ambitions, but everyday life has got in the way and they are settling for a life that they don't want. The only things to look forward to are holidays and retirement.

OVERTHINKING

People are exhausting themselves through overthinking, always worrying about 'What if'. We are constantly bombarded with information via emails, texts and social media, which means that we're subjected to more bad news stories than ever before.

Overthinking happens because people are processing what they're exposed to and looking for solutions, ways that they can feel safe and secure and for their futures to be certain.

This need for certainty creates a fear of the unknown and they become stuck. The focus becomes the things that have gone wrong in the past. They worry what other people will think and compare their lives to how they perceive other people's lives to be; often doing what they think is expected of them rather than what they really want to do.

The paralysis of analysis describes when people's minds are full of clutter and they're unable to switch off and be creative. This results in a double bind. Contrast that to when people have fresh minds. This is when ideas pop into their heads. All of this means that overthinking is one of the major things keeping you stuck in the place where you don't want to be.

Kids' thinking is very simplistic. While adults are looking for happiness, kids find contentment in the moment.

PROCRASTINATING

'Don't follow your dreams, grab them by the scruff of the neck and do or be them.' This is a quote from one of the kids we spoke to. It sums up the attitude that kids take.

What happens to those dreams that you had as a kid as you become an adult? How do you lose that passion, fun and fulfilment and, more importantly, when do you accept that it's okay to live life like this?

There are several reasons why you lose sight of your dreams. They include overwhelm and feeling out of control, fear, losing our way and not being clear on what we want, lack of time and lack of energy.

However, one of the biggest reasons is procrastination. People put off doing the very things that they need to do in order to get themselves unstuck and moving forward. Kids just do things. Adults 'try' and do things, and as you know the great philosopher Yoda said: 'There is no try, there is only do or do not'. Having intention isn't actually doing anything.

Procrastination originates from a lack of motivation. If you enjoy something then it happens easily. Adults lose their 'Why' for doing what they are doing, and therefore lose their purpose in life. They put goals in place just so they can be ticked off and there is often no real desire to achieve them, which is why many goals are not completed.

Having purpose is a natural motivator, you just need to reconnect with your own purpose in life. It's your own natural motivator and when you do that life becomes purposeful and easy again.

PASSENGER OR DRIVER?

One of the themes that we noticed from our research that prevents people from living the life they want, is that they surrender control of their lives to other people. In other words, they are the passenger rather than the driver in their lives.

People are reluctant to take responsibility for themselves and are quick to blame others for their lack of advancement. They seek quick and easy solutions that require the minimum effort and look to manifest what they want from life. There's nothing wrong with using the law of attraction, but you need to take the right action and be prepared to do what it takes.

Why do people continue to take the easy options, and remain passengers in their lives when it's clearly not getting them the outcomes that they want? Lack of self-belief is one reason. For example, if you hear yourself saying that you 'can't' do something, it's a sure sign of a self-limiting belief and is completely disempowering.

Turning that around and asking yourself, 'How you can do it' instead completely changes your mindset. If it's something that you really don't want to do, be honest with yourself and acknowledge that it's a choice not to do it. That will change your mindset to driver rather than passenger.

We want you to reconnect with those amazing resources that you had as a kid when you were learning to walk, talk, ride a bike, swim, and to re-engage with those resources of persistence and determination to achieve the things that you want to achieve as an adult.

If you're encouraging your own children to push themselves to achieve, what kind of role model are you to them? Are you prepared to do the same in your own life?

PART II—REDISCOVERING YOU

IF YOU DON'T LIKE IT, DON'T DO IT

We tend to think that age and experience make us better people, but what if acting like an adult is what leads to us feeling more unhappy and less effective? What if reconnecting with your inner kid is the key to not only inner contentment but also success in life, better friendships and relationships, and generally feeling more fulfilled?

We're not saying that kids do everything right, nor that everyone had a wonderful childhood as that isn't the case. What we are saying is that as adults we have lost some of the resources that came easily to us when we were growing up. These are resources that you can reconnect with and use, in combination with the knowledge and experience that you've gained as an adult, to get the outcomes that you want in life.

Kids will only do the things that they enjoy, if they don't want to do something they will say so. Adults 'suffer in silence' and continue to do things that they really don't want to do. They do this for a number of reasons, including through guilt and not wanting to offend. Experiencing long-term inner conflict like this can create dis-ease within the body.

YOU THINK TOO MUCH

Kids take things literally. As we grow up, many people develop an inferential communication style. By that we mean that they begin to apply their own meaning to the words they hear rather than taking them literally as they were spoken and intended by the speaker.

This can create all sorts of issues as most people who do this will apply a negative meaning to what they hear, reflecting the beliefs that they hold about themselves.

You have to learn to identify the words that are actually being spoken and separate them from the meaning that you're applying, realising that applied meaning is just a mind read based upon your own model of the world. This will assist you with relearning the Art & Science of Underthinking that kids do so easily.

BEING REAL

Adults create stress within themselves through not being real, or in other words not being themselves. They often behave as one person at work and another at home or with their friends.

Kids forgive quickly and forget easily, whereas adults hold onto grudges, sometimes for a lifetime. Rather than express how they are feeling, they pretend they have moved on, only to throw the old disagreements back into the ring sometimes years later.

Kids don't care what people think; if they are thinking something, they will say it. Adults bite their tongue, which leads to a build-up of resentment and other negative emotions, causing dis-ease and lowering of the immune system.

If we do as kids do, we'll improve our emotional and physical wellbeing. That means accepting ourselves as we are, continuing to do the things that we enjoy doing regardless of what anyone else thinks (or what we think they think!), and being real and true to ourselves.

OKAY WITH NOT BEING OKAY

Life is full of ups and downs and there will be times when you're not okay, and that's fine ... as long as it's short term and not the norm. Examine the reasons why you are not okay, is it a temporary situation?

There are many reasons why adults are not okay when they're not in a temporary situation, which we covered in this chapter.

If not being okay has been long term for you, examine the reason, and then the reason behind that reason ... and then the reason behind that reason. This can give you some real insights into the things that you have been ignoring consciously. Addressing these and taking the right action will assist you with regaining that pure joy of life that kids experience on a regular basis.

PART III-UNCONDITIONAL LOVE

CONTENTMENT VS. HAPPINESS

As a kid, we find contentment in the moment, in whatever it is that we are doing, and the more simple the activity the more we enjoy it. As we grow up, we are programmed to become consumers, to look for happiness outside of ourselves and to base our achievement of happiness on what we have or do not have in our lives.

Adults perceive happiness as something to strive for, rather than a feeling that we can access at any time.

What is this elusive happiness that everyone is looking for? When you reconnect with your inner kid you experience peace of mind and inner contentment, and realise that this is what you have been looking for all along, and that ironically it was within you all the time.

All you need to do is unlearn some of the habits and ways of thinking that you've taken onboard whilst growing up and relearn how to experience inner contentment within yourself.

BEYOND POSITIVE THINKING

Kids have such a sunny outlook on life because they haven't yet taken on beliefs that belong to other people. They believe they can be anything that they want to be, and do anything they want to do.

Adults place imaginary chains around themselves, which limit what they believe they are capable of doing or achieving.

All learning, change and behaviour takes place at the unconscious level; which is why it takes more than just positive thinking to create permanent change.

The root cause of the problem needs to be addressed at the unconscious level, as do any unconscious reasons for holding onto old behaviours. Along with this, you also need to carry out the right actions; as thinking positively alone will not get you the outcomes you want.

THE POWER OF IMAGINATION

Many people believe that they don't have a choice about how they think, feel or even behave, that it just happens.

If you are always playing out worst-case scenarios in your mind, that just means you have trained your mind to think in this way and you can retrain your mind to think differently.

Your unconscious mind doesn't know the difference between what is real and what is imagined, so consider the unnecessary stress you are imposing upon yourself and your body on a regular basis by seeing everything turn out badly ... when the event hasn't even happened!

Instead, create an image of the event turning out successfully and every time you think about that event, make sure you are focusing on this positive image that you have created. Over a period of time you will retrain your brain to use your wonderful imagination to support your general wellbeing, which will attract positive opportunities. You will be in a much better frame of mind to notice those opportunities and to be able to act on them if you wish.

PART IV-PUTTING YOURSELF FIRST

HOW TO ADAPT TO ANY SITUATION

Being able to adapt to any situation is one way of achieving win–win outcomes. Having only one way of thinking keeps you stuck with no options, if you have just two ways of thinking that creates a dilemma, either or, and neither way may be appropriate or conversely both ways may work. This creates the paralysis of analysis.

Where people are unsure, they won't do anything at all. The key is to notice many ways to get your outcome and have the flexibility to be able to take the option that is the best at that time.

Kids have natural adaptability due to their excitement and curiosity, with no preconceived ideas of how things should turn out. Routine and structure is put in place by parents, which ensures that kids have the holistic environment they need to thrive (i.e. adequate food, water, sleep, rest, stimulation and activities, so they are at their best mentally and physically). They have persistence and determination. Rather than 'trying' to do things, they just do them.

There are a number of things that prevent people from having this flexibility as adults, which we explored in this chapter.

Taking on board the suggestions that we have given in the chapter will greatly enhance your ability to remain flexible and allow you to get your outcomes whilst assisting others to get their outcomes too.

THE ART OF MANIPULATION

Kids naturally put themselves first. As we grow up we're discouraged from acting upon what we want to do for ourselves and instead told that we should put everyone else's desires, thoughts and wishes before our own.

This can become a way of life, often to our own detriment. What you need to do instead is look for win–win outcomes. You have to break the habit of saying 'Yes' to things when you are really thinking 'No'.

Remember that kids only do things that they want to do. Using this skill that kids utilise so readily (i.e. the art of manipulation) in a positive way as an adult will assist you with putting yourself first in a way that works for you, whilst still being a win–win for everyone else.

You'll also identify where there is no win–win and can decide to walk away from a situation or relationship.

LOST DREAMS

It's too easy to get caught up in day-to-day life, in that list of tasks that you never seem to get to the bottom of.

Kids are full of possibility, while adults lose sight of the things that they believed were once possible because of necessity and the list of things they feel obliged to do.

There will never be a right time. Instead of waiting for things to become easier, seize the opportunity now and reconnect with your lost dreams.

PART V – THERE'S LIGHT AT THE END OF THE TUNNEL (AND IT'S NOT ANOTHER TRAIN)

MUM KNOWS BEST

It could sound as though all of the unconscious programming that you were exposed to as you were growing up was negative. But this isn't so. You also received lots of positive programming and were given lots of positive resources that are often outside of your awareness.

Think back to some of the phrases that your parents and grandparents used on a regular basis and revisit them as an adult. What do those phrases really mean and what useful resources can you take from them now?

JUST FOR FUN

While some people lose touch with their inner kid as they grow into adults, there are others who continue to retain a youthful approach to life, throughout their life, regardless of age.

These people are fun to be around and easily get on with people. When we like being around people, we're more likely to go out of our way to help them, and they us. In this spirit of cooperation, win–win outcomes are more easily achieved.

It's useful to think about the traits that these people retain, so that you can adopt these characteristics yourself.

Having fun has all sorts of positive health benefits. Getting in touch with your inner kid and finding a way to make even the most mundane tasks enjoyable will reap the benefits in all areas of your life. What could be more enjoyable and easier than having fun whilst improving your life for the better?

IT'S RIGHT FOR RIGHT NOW

Even though you might want change, sometimes you don't know what you actually want. It's often easier to know what you don't want.

It might also feel as though you're not changing as quickly as you'd like to.

Believing that there is an end destination or that there is something that you should 'be' is flawed thinking. There is no one 'right' way and waiting for this right way to appear prevents people from moving forward and keeps them stuck. The most important thing is to set off and see where your journey takes you, knowing that each stage is 'right for right now' and that you will learn and grow as you move forward.

Kids don't plan ahead. They enjoy what they are doing in the moment and as an adult you can reconnect with this way of thinking, which will help you develop the mindset that is supportive for making the changes that you want to make.

PART VI-THE ART & SCIENCE OF UNDERTHINKING

We've said that reconnecting with your inner kid and related way of thinking can greatly assist you. But exactly what thinking are we talking about reconnecting with?

In many respects, it's the opposite to the way most adults think. We've identified four principles that make up the Art & Science of Underthinking.

PRINCIPLE 1-KEEPING IT SIMPLE

Kids do things purely because they want to.

Reassess the things that you spend your valuable time doing and what you spend your hard-earned money on. The aim is to simplify areas where you overcomplicate things unnecessarily. This will give you the opportunity to make changes so that life is more enjoyable and fun. Who says that things have to be done in a conventional way?

Utilising the Art & Science of Underthinking will free up your thinking and give you the best conditions to come up with amazing ideas to enhance your life for the better.

PRINCIPLE 2-IT'S NOT PERSONAL

When something happens as an adult, often we hold on to what has happened, sometimes for a lifetime. Mind reading what someone else may be thinking or the motive behind their actions can be exhausting. Second-guessing like this will influence how you behave, interact and communicate, at the very least impacting negatively upon your peace of mind and inner contentment.

Choosing not to take things personally allows you to remain flexible and respond to situations appropriately rather than reacting.

Remind yourself that 'It's not personal' and refocus on something positive that's worth focusing on!

PRINCIPLE 3-BE EXCITED

Kids get really excited on a regular basis and this is something that seems to fade as you become an adult.

One of the main reasons for this is that adults often don't feel that they have anything to get excited about. Everyday life can be boring, which can affect your energy levels. You then don't feel that you have the motivation to lift yourself out of your day-to-day routine.

Excitement is a really powerful positive emotion. When you feel excited you release all sorts of happy hormones. Being excited is really motivating and leads you to take positive action because you want to feel that way again.

Reconnecting with your inner kid, and becoming excited again, will enable you to access that feeling of sheer joy that you can too easily lose touch with as you leave childhood.

PRINCIPLE 4-PLAY MORE

There are many studies that have been carried out that highlight the importance of spontaneous play both for children and adults.

Benefits include reducing stress, promoting relaxation, increasing creativity, boosting imagination and enhancing problem-solving skills.

When playing you become lost in the moment. It can also increase productivity at work, as well as building and enhancing relationships.

There are so many ways that you can play. All you need to do is find something that you enjoy, fully engage and lose yourself completely in what you're doing.

BE MORE KID: HOW TO ESCAPE THE GROWN UP TRAP AND LIVE LIFE TO THE FULL

After reading this book, we hope that you're able to recognise the natural resources you once had as a kid and reconnect with all these resources that are still within you.

Doing this will allow you to be more resilient to the inevitable challenges that come your way in life.

Remember that it's never too late to change your life. The starting point is the desire to do so. By reconnecting with your inner kid and utilising the examples and exercises that we've given you in this book, you can live the life you once imagined and that you deserve.

We've given you the tools, now it's up to you to take action. You have to take responsibility for yourself and understand that no-one is going to do this for you.

We've opened the door to this world of possibility, now it's up to you to take the first step and walk through it.

WHERE TO GO NEXT

We don't want this book to sit on a shelf gathering dust. We want you to use the exercises, concepts and themes we've shared to make your life better. Be more kid!

You'll find additional resources and support, including information about events and training courses that we're running at www.be-more-kid.com. Join the Be More Kid revolution – we can't wait to see you there!

EXERCISE GLOSSARY

Chapter 12
How to get rid of negative emotion - p. 112
The keys to being able to adapt to any situation - p. 114

Chapter 13
How to start saying No - p. 120

Chapter 14
Reconnecting with your inner kid and remembering lost dreams - p. 131

Chapter 16
How do you answer the question, 'How are you?' - p. 150
Find your fun - p. 152

Chapter 18
Where can you make life more simple? - p. 169

Chapter 21
Finding ways to play more - p. 189

NLP GLOSSARY

Accessing Cues
External signs that give us information about what we do inside. The signs include breathing, gestures, posture and eye patterns.

Anchoring
The NLP technique whereby a stimulus is linked to a response. An anchor can be intentional or naturally occurring.

'As-If' Frame
Acting 'as if' something were true. That is, pretending that you are competent at something when you are not, like tennis. The idea is that the pretence will increase your capability.

Associated
It is related to your relationship to an experience. In a memory, for example, you are associated when you are looking through your own eyes, and experiencing the auditory and kinaesthetic at the same time.

Auditory
Hearing and sounds.

Behaviour
Any externally verifiable activity we engage in.

Beliefs
Generalisations we make about the world and our opinions about it. Connected to our values.

Calibration
Involves the comparison between two different sets of non-verbal cues.

Congruence
When the externally verifiable behaviour matches the words the person says.

Conscious
That of which we are currently aware.

Dissociated
Deals with your relationship to an experience. In a memory, for example, you are dissociated when you are not looking through your own eyes, and you see your body in the picture.

Downtime
Downtime occurs whenever we go inside. It can occur when we go internal for a piece of information or when we get in touch with our feelings (see also Uptime).

Ecology
In NLP, ecology is the study of consequences. We are interested in the results of any change that occurs. It is often useful to look at the ecology in making any change as to the consequences for self, family (or business), society and planet.

Elicitation
Inducing a state or gathering information by asking questions or observing behaviour.

Frame
A frame sets a context, which is a way we can make a distinction about something, as in 'As-If' Frame, Backtrack Frame, Outcome Frame.

Future Pace
Mentally rehearsing a future result to install a new strategy so that the desired outcome occurs.

Gustatory
Taste.

Incongruence
When the externally verifiable behaviour does not match the words the person says.

Intent
The purpose or objective of a behaviour.

Internal Representations
The content of our thinking, which includes pictures, sounds, feelings, tastes, smells and self-talk. How we represent the external world internally.

Kinaesthetic
This sense includes feelings and sensations.

Law of Requisite Variety
The Law of Requisite Variety states: 'In a given physical system, that part of the system with the greatest flexibility of behaviour will control the system.'

Meta Position
Sometimes also called the Third Position. A dissociated position to view something in an objective way.

Metaphor
A story (analogy or figure of speech) told with a purpose, which allows us to bypass the conscious resistance of the client and have the client make connections at a deeper level.

Modal Operator
The modal operator relates to words, which form the rules of our lives. Modal operators of necessity relate to words such as should, must, have to. Modal operators of possibility relate to words that denote that which is considered possible or impossible such as can, cannot.

Model
In NLP, a model is a description of a concept or a behaviour, which includes the strategies, filter patterns and physiology so as to be able to be adopted easily.

Model of the World
A person's values, beliefs and attitudes that relate to and create their own world.

Neuro Linguistic Programming (NLP)
NLP is the study of excellence, which describes how our thinking produces our behaviour, and allows us to model excellence and to reproduce that behaviour.

Olfactory
The sense of smell.

Outcome
Desired result. A goal.

Perceptual Position
Describes our point of view in a specific situation. First position is our own point of view. Second position is usually someone else's point of view. Third position is the point of view of a dissociated observer.

Phobia
A severe, associated, unwanted response of fear regarding some person or event in the past.

Preferred Rep System
This is the representational system that someone most often uses to think, learn and organise their experiences.

Representation
A thought in the mind, which can be comprised of Visual, Auditory, Kinaesthetic, Olfactory (smell), Gustatory (taste) and Auditory Digital (self-talk).

Representational System
One of the six things you can do in your mind: Visual (pictures), Auditory (sounds), Kinaesthetic (feelings), Olfactory (smell), Gustatory (taste) and Auditory Digital (self-talk).

Resourceful State
This refers to any state where a person has positive, helpful emotions and strategies available to them. The state implies a successful outcome.

Resources
Resources are the means to create change within oneself or to accomplish an outcome. Resources may include certain states, adopting specific physiology, new strategies, beliefs, values or attitudes, even specific behaviour.

State
Relates to our internal emotional condition. That is, a happy state, a sad state, a motivated state, etc. In NLP we believe that the state determines our results, and so we are careful to be in states of excellence.

Unconscious
That of which you are not conscious, or which is out of awareness.

Unconscious Mind
The part of your mind that you are not conscious of ... everything that is not conscious right now.

Uptime
A state where attention is focused on the outside (see also Downtime).

Values
High-level generalisations describing that which is important to you – in NLP sometimes called criteria. They are what we are willing to spend our time on, what motivate us, and what we move either towards or away from.

Visual
Having to do with the sense of sight. Pictures.

ABOUT THE AUTHORS

Mark and Nicky Taylor are professional Behaviour and Relationship Experts. After meeting in 2006, and realising that they share a common passion for making a positive difference in people's lives, they explored how they could create a meaningful life together in a way that would also benefit other people. In 2009 they chose to train in neuro-linguistic programming (NLP) and related disciplines and started coaching others, assisting them to make huge changes in their lives.

If you are not familiar with NLP, it's a group of models that come from various sources such as behavioural psychology. NLP incorporates the work of the family therapist Virginia Satir, Gestalt therapist Fritz Perls – and Milton Erickson, who is considered by many to be the father of modern hypnotherapy.

So, amazed by the positive results that they were getting with their clients, by the end of 2009 they found themselves in Sydney, Australia, training as Trainers, so that they could increase the positive impact that they were having.

Continuing their own personal evolution, they continued their studies and qualified as Master Trainers in 2015, the highest level of NLP. In 2018 they both qualified as Master Trainers of Hypnosis. They are the only couple in the world to have qualified together at this level with the American Board of NLP and the American Board of Hypnosis.

Since 2009, they have made a difference to thousands of people's lives across the globe.

Ed James is a broadcaster, live event host, businessman and NLP Master Practitioner – having first trained with Mark and Nicky in 2016. He's always had a passion for self-improvement, an obsession with how successful people do what they do and a desire to study and take learnings from those who are clearly the leaders in their fields. As a broadcaster on Heart, he's spoken to literally thousands of listeners over the 18 years of hosting a live, daily radio show and evolved and adapted to remain relevant within the changing industry landscape. In 2017 he co-founded a full service content marketing agency: HDY Agency. Based in Digbeth, Birmingham's buzzy creative quarter, the agency services national and global clients to help them tell their story to reach new customers. 'Implementing the learnings from 'Be More Kid' they have successfully developed a culture of trust, creativity and fun where they are never afraid to ask questions and challenge the status quo. One of his driving mantras is, ' If the thought of something scares you – you should do it!' This has led him to appear on stage in a musical (when he can't sing), conquer the Three Peaks challenge and jump out of a plane for charity.

INDEX